D0949507

The Tao *of* Self-Confidence

The Tao *of* Self-Confidence

A GUIDE TO MOVING BEYOND TRAUMA AND AWAKENING THE LEADER WITHIN

Sheena Yap Chan

WILEY

Published by John Wiley & Sons, Inc., Hoboken, New Jersey.
Published simultaneously in Canada.

For general information on our other products and services or for technical support, please contact our Customer Care Department within the United States at (800) 762-2974, outside the United States at (317) 572-3993 or fax (317) 572-4002.

Wiley also publishes its books in a variety of electronic formats. Some content that appears in print may not be available in electronic formats. For more information about Wiley products, visit our web site at www.wiley.com.

Library of Congress Cataloging-in-Publication Data:

Names: Chan, Sheena Yap, author.
Title: The tao of self-confidence : a guide to moving beyond trauma and
awakening the leader within / Sheena Yap Chan.
Description: Hoboken, New Jersey : Wiley, [2023] | Includes index.
Identifiers: LCCN 2022056044 (print) | LCCN 2022056045 (ebook) | ISBN
9781394166572 (hardback) | ISBN 9781394166596 (adobe pdf) | ISBN
9781394166589 (epub)
Subjects: LCSH: Leadership in women. | Asian American women. |
Self-confidence.
Classification: LCC HQ1233 .C395 2023 (print) | LCC HQ1233 (ebook) | DDC
303.3/4082--dc23/eng/20230110
LC record available at https://lccn.loc.gov/2022056044
LC ebook record available at https://lccn.loc.gov/2022056045

Cover design: Paul McCarthy
Cover image: © Getty Images | Wilatlak Villette

SKY10045203_033023

Contents

Introduction: The State of Asian Women

Growing up in Toronto, Canada, in the 1990s, it was always difficult for me to see anyone in the media who looked like me. No one had similar facial features, and I found it hard to accept who I was and my own culture. I wished for blond hair and blue eyes. I wanted to change my name from Sheena to Heather to sound more "Western." Can you imagine being 9 years old and already facing all kinds of self-esteem issues because people who looked like me weren't represented in what I saw and heard every day?

Over the years, I've worked on fully accepting myself and my heritage. In the process, I promised myself that I would always try to create a stronger representation for Asian women in order to dismantle the negative stereotypes that we still face today.

I started a podcast in 2015 called *The Tao of Self-Confidence* where I interviewed more than 700 Asian women on the topic of confidence. Although my podcast has reached over 1.2 million downloads and is among the top 0.5% most popular podcasts in the world, the visibility factor for Asian women was still non-existent almost everywhere else.

In 2021, I co-created a book called *Asian Women Who BossUp*, which highlights the stories of 18 Asian women who have been able to forge their own paths, overcome obstacles, and thrive. It was amazing to see 16 Asian women on the front cover of the book—something I've never seen before.

Asian Women Who BossUp started giving us the visibility we deserve, and Asian women were seen in a different light. For years, Asian women have been "bossing up" in their own industries, but no publication has highlighted their collective breakthroughs and insight until now.

I always believe that if you want the representation you crave, it must start with you. If you're not out there trying to create the representation you want to see, you're unknowingly continuing the vicious cycle.

A report from Catalyst.org (n.d.) on the representation of women of color in management and leadership roles in the United States in 2021 was particularly disappointing, although not surprising:

- Black women, 4.4%
- Hispanic women, 4.3%
- Asian women, 2.7%

When I saw the stats, I started to wonder why Asian women had the lowest representation in leadership roles. Something in me wanted to dig deep and figure out why this was happening.

When I was presented with this opportunity to write this book, I felt a little hesitant. I had bouts of imposter syndrome, doubting I was even the *right* person to write it. Who was I to write a book based on the topic of leadership? But I realized that if I gave in to my doubts and fears and didn't write this book, I would've been the biggest hypocrite in the world. So I went for it. I found a way to overcome my emotional blocks and made it happen.

I feel grateful and honored to have this chance to write a book that not only helps Asian women but all women in leadership. As women, we still face so many challenges in this arena.

Many leadership books I see out there are basic how-to books or rigid manuals. Most of them don't talk about the reasons why women, particularly Asian women, don't advance in leadership. So I decided to create a book that really dove into the cultural and historical issues that affect a leadership career. That means exploring the things we have gone through, including what came before us, our heritage, the moment we were born into, and how that has affected us in our daily life.

We don't realize that our personal history and experiences can linger in us and subconsciously affect our actions and decisions in our daily lives. These subconscious, forgotten life experiences may be part of the reason why you are struggling in your current situation.

This is why I decided to write a book like no other, a book I wished had been around when I was starting out: a book on leadership that touches on historical and cultural mindsets as well as personal roadblocks or trauma you may be going through. If you don't work on your mindset first or figure out what kind of baggage you're carrying from the past, it's going to be an uphill battle to become the effective leader you were meant to be.

This book will tackle the things that you don't normally talk about: the taboos in your culture and how you were brought up. I will bring up things that your Asian parents will tell you not to talk about. I will take you on a journey that you have never experienced before.

This book will tackle topics such as the model minority myth and how that has affected the Asian community for decades, the many issues that Asian women still face today, intergenerational trauma, how to unlock other forms of trauma, the journey to healing from your traumas, self-love and why it matters, the power of self-confidence, and the future of Asian women leadership.

And while this book may seem like it's catering to a specific audience, these specific stories complete a narrative tapestry that helps all of us better understand each other. You can learn from this because there will be parts of my story that you can relate to. I'm sure you have different taboos in your culture or negative stereotypes that make you feel like less than a leader. I'm sure you've had to navigate issues with racism or sexism in your life simply by being a woman.

It's important to share your specific stories. I've been rejected way too many times in my life because my story was "too specific" or that it catered to a "specific" audience. But your specific story can help people from all walks of life in many ways. You can either relate to a story, learn something new, or see things from a different perspective.

If you hear the same stories over and over, how would you learn and create positive changes? You can't keep doing the same things and expect a different result (which, by the way, is the very definition of insanity).

Being "specific" is a good thing, and it's about time to learn about leadership from a different perspective, especially one that's often seen as invisible or not taken seriously in leadership roles: that perspective is from me, a woman of Asian descent.

Stereotypes come up just from how I look: the media has often implied people who look like me were the cause of COVID-19 or that my only goal is to be a good housewife. Because of my Asian features, I face immediate judgment, and this judgment from stereotypes has fueled a rise of violence against Asian women like me, especially since the COVID-19 pandemic. The community has been in tears for the Atlanta shooting in 2021 that took the lives of six innocent Asian women; the death of

Christina Yuna Lee, who was murdered in her own apartment; and many others.

Having a leadership book from an Asian woman's perspective is more important than ever. Being on the receiving end of generations of misdirected hate and rage, voices like mine need to come out of the background and be heard. In the words of Lizzo: "*It's about damn time!*"

1

The Model Minority Myth and How That Affects Us

THE ASIAN COMMUNITY has always been seen as silent, well-behaved achievers and held up as "good examples" when talking about the underrepresented and immigrants in Western countries, especially the United States. While it may seem like a compliment, this stereotype has caused harm that's rippled through the Asian community.

According to the book, *The Routledge Companion to Race and Ethnicity*: "*The term 'model minority' refers to minority groups that have ostensibly achieved a high level of success in contemporary US society. The term has been used most often to describe Asian Americans, a group seen as having attained educational and financial success relative to other immigrant groups. The 'model minority' label on its surface seems to be an accolade because it appears to praise Asian Americans for their achievements.*"[1]

And yet you rarely see Asian women (or even men) in higher leadership and management roles. In many instances, the measure of success for Asians is taken for granted. For example, how can one Asian person in a leadership position be seen as a "success" in representation? It's as if that person's Asian-ness was enough to represent the more than 24 million Asian Americans who live in the United States.

You would think that if Asian Americans "achieved a high level of success," then at the bare minimum, the community would represent at least 20% of the leadership positions in the United States, which is far from the reality.

History of the Term "Model Minority"

On January 9, 1966, sociologist William Petersen wrote an article for *The New York Times Magazine* called, "Success Story: Japanese-American Style."[2]

In the original article, Petersen talks about the exclusion, challenges, and discrimination that Japanese Americans had gone through and mentions how they successfully overcame their challenges by assimilating in to Western culture.

While some Japanese Americans embraced this article as a success for the community in terms of gaining visibility and validation, most of them thought the depiction of Japanese Americans as "compliant" was overly exaggerated.[3]

It's amazing how one person's article has drastically affected the way Asian Americans and Canadians were seen by the Western world. It's taken as absolute truth, when in reality, it's only one person's perspective.

Japanese Americans started to be used as an example of obedience and strong work ethic compared to the "problem minority."

If there is one word to abolish using to describe non-white people it's the word "minority."

In many cases, it no longer means the statistical minority, but a term for exclusion and inferiority: minor as in not important or not the preferred norm. "Minority" feels like we're being downgraded because of differences in cultural background. It's become such a problematic term that needs to be dismantled in the work for equity and progress.

Since that article came out from Petersen claiming that Japanese Americans were the model minority, more articles came out claiming Asian Americans are the model minority because we are "obedient" and willing to assimilate in to Western culture.

From personal experience, I think this is especially true for Chinese Americans, as mentioned in this follow-up article titled: "Success of One Minority Group in the US."[4]

The article describes Chinese Americans as hardworking and self-sufficient people who don't need help from anyone else to achieve the American Dream. It also mentions that even with low pay and long hours building the railroad tracks, and faced with the Chinese Exclusion Act, Chinese Americans "never complained" about it. Chinese Americans were willing to take any job they could get in America. If they were a scholar in their home country and the only job they could get in America was being a waiter, then they were willing to take it. The message was that you could throw anything at Chinese Americans, and no matter how bad the situation, they would find a way to adapt.

The Danger of the Myth

The Western world has always lumped the Asian community together as one race and one culture in spite of the fact that Asian culture is a very diverse community with many different ethnicities.

Even when I googled the terms "Asian Culture Facts," the top-ranked article that popped up was "10 Interesting Facts to Help You Understand Chinese Culture" showing two white people in traditional Chinese clothing.[5]

It's 2022, and the world according to Google still thinks that all Asians come from China. Hopefully, by the time you read this book, the algorithms have changed and will rank an article that has diverse representation when you search for "Asian Culture Facts."

This has become a huge problem, especially with the rise of Anti-Asian hate crimes in the United States and Canada. When former US President Donald Trump constantly called the COVID-19 virus the "China Virus,"[6] it became a call to violence, and every single Asian person inadvertently became a target of a hate crime.

I remember reading articles of Asian elderly men and women, whether it was Chinese, Thai, Filipino, or Indian, being attacked. Each time, I couldn't help thinking that it could've been my mother, grandmother, or aunt who was attacked. Even people in the Latinx community were being attacked whenever they were mistaken for an Asian person. I remember reading an article about a 70-year-old Mexican woman who was brutally beaten up while riding the bus for that reason.[7]

In 2020, mainstream media started publishing and televising news of the COVID-19 virus, mentioning its origin in Wuhan, China, and sensationalizing speculations instead of focusing on facts. Whether I wanted to or not, I felt even more afraid for my safety every time I had to go out:

- One look at me, and it's an instant assumption that I was the cause of COVID-19.
- People might assume I was a bat eater even though I have never eaten a bat, and I haven't eaten meat for more than 5 years.
- People might tell me to "Go back to China!" even though I have never been to China and was born in the Philippines.
- I was constantly afraid my family might become a target of all the misplaced anger and hate over the pandemic.

And when I reflect on it now, I realize this was the same fear and paranoia that our community has dealt with for being the scapegoat for the COVID-19 pandemic.

It's difficult to be seen as a community of diverse backgrounds when physical appearance and stereotypes lump Asians as a monolith culture. But here's the truth:

- Forty-nine sovereign countries make up Asia.[8]
- As of 2022, more than 4.7 billion people live in Asia, which is considered the most populous continent in the world.
- Asia has more than 2,300 recognized languages.

The model minority myth started the ball rolling on reducing Asians to one or two cultures. The mindset that how one or a few behave represents the whole culture has negatively affected generations of the Asian community, especially Asian women.

An article from the *Epoch Times* talks about taking a closer look behind the rise of Anti-Asian hate crimes. I was a contributor to that article, and I mentioned that the model minority was a big reason for this rise, especially for Asian women. I mentioned how the model minority myth dehumanizes Asian women, even today:

> *Women are less likely to report a crime due to our upbringing. When something traumatic happens, we usually keep it to ourselves or ignore that it happened. Also, growing up in an Asian culture, we want to save face and never tarnish the family name even when we know that traumatic experience wasn't our fault.... We end up being the easy target.*[9]

The perception that Asians are achievers, model citizens, and self-sufficient can hurt rather than help. As an Asian, if you're seen to ask for help from our peers or failed to live to a certain standard, you'd end up becoming a "failure" to our culture according to the standards of the Western world. The pressure is high when you have to live by these unrealistic standards.

If you end up speaking up or talking back, you become the problematic Asian woman, and you're not living by the standards of our cultural upbringing. You end up being penalized for not living up to the expected stereotype. You're supposed to be the model citizen who should never complain about any injustice that you face because the older generation never complained about anything when they migrated to the United States and Canada.

Even asking a question feels like you've failed as a human being because you're supposed to be the high achiever who knows everything and should never have to ask for help. How many times have you wanted to raise your hand up in school or at work to ask a question but are too embarrassed to do it, because you fear that you will get laughed at or someone might call you stupid? Been there, done that many times in my life.

Even as we saw a rise of anti-Asian hate crimes during the pandemic, it didn't start there. There's a long history of racism against Asians, which I will explain in the next chapters.

Mainstream media hardly ever covered the racist attacks that happened to our community in the beginning of the Stop Asian Hate Movement. Social media platforms like Twitter and Instagram were the source of most of the news about the attacks against the Asian community.

The Atlanta shooting that happened on March 16, 2021, which took the lives of six Asian women, was the moment that mainstream media started to talk about the rise of anti-Asian hate crimes.

The Model Minority Myth and Mental Health

I wanted to have this as a separate topic because mental health is not talked about enough, especially in the Asian community. When it comes to mental health, the model minority myth has definitely made it almost impossible for you to talk about how you feel or even seek help. The *Huffington Post* article titled "7 Ways 'The Model Minority' Myth Hurts Asian American's Mental Health"[10] was one of the few examples that sheds light on what the community is going through. It listed these very real concerns:

1. **The expectations for academic and career success can feel impossible to meet.** You are always seen as hardworking, intelligent, and nice. The pressure and anxiety start to increase when you cannot live up to this standard, especially when it comes to academics. When you become a B or C student, you've become a failure to yourself, your family, and your culture.
2. **The myth suggests Asian Americans face less racism than other people of color.** Asian Americans have been facing racism for centuries but were told to never talk about it. Mainstream Western history also tend to erase or gloss over major events that disadvantaged Asian Americans, such as the Chinese Exclusion Act or the Japanese internment camps. Many people also assume that anti-Asian racism didn't exist in other countries during the pandemic. I can tell you, being in Canada, that this is far from the truth.
3. **The model minority myth hides the economic realities of many Asian Americans.** Asians are often portrayed as an affluent group. Often, this harms the many others who need resources and help.
4. **They're less likely to seek out mental health help.** This is so true; mental health has always been a taboo in the community. You are told to never share your feelings, and it's a sign of weakness, especially if you go to a licensed therapist. Being able to express what you are feeling is healthy for you to maintain your mental well-being.

5. **Not all Asians are considered model minority enough.** If you don't live up to a certain standard, you end up being a failure, just like when I failed kindergarten in the Philippines for coloring outside the lines. I was considered a failure from the age of 5 and this mentality carried with me until my late 30s.
6. **They fall into careers and fields they're disinterested in.** I was told that getting a 9-to-5 job was the path to success. So I did what I was told and for 12 years I worked in an office thinking that was the highest level of success I was able to attain as an Asian woman. Even though something inside me knew that I couldn't picture myself working in an office until I retired, I continued to work there because that's what the meaning of success was. So many people end up working a career they hate, but they stay because of this belief.
7. **It distances people from their culture.** As a child, I wanted to have blond hair and blue eyes and change my name to Heather because I wanted to be more Caucasian. I thought that was the standard of beauty, and I was embarrassed of being Asian. Even when I lived in the Philippines, it was always about assimilating in to American culture. Everyone wanted to speak English well and follow the trends of the Western world.

As an Asian woman, it feels like your whole life is laid out for you. You go to school, graduate, get a good job, get married, have kids, and never rock the boat. Anything outside of that is considered unsuccessful or shameful. The judgments start coming out once you start doing something outside of the path that was laid out for you, and you feel like something is wrong with you because you want to forge your own path.

Even if you want to seek professional help, such as going to see a therapist, it is seen by your culture as a sign of weakness, and it means that something is wrong with you even when every person goes through some form of mental health challenges, myself included.

Now, I am not a licensed mental health expert, and I don't claim to be. I am an advocate to normalize mental health because the taboos in the culture are hurting people, especially during the pandemic. When you had to deal with the lockdown and the anti-Asian racism at the same time, of course your mental health would be affected. It's okay to say you are not okay.

I personally was not okay in the beginning of the lockdown. I honestly thought it was the end of the world when everything shut down. It felt like there was no reason to live, and I was too afraid to tell anyone that I was going through my own mental health challenges. It's never healthy to keep in your struggles and feelings. You are like a ticking time bomb that is ready to explode, and that's never a good thing.

Interviewing more than 700 Asian women on my podcast, it was a breath of fresh air to hear that I wasn't the only one dealing with mental health issues. Knowing that they found different outlets to express their true feelings made me feel like I was not alone in my journey and that we are all in this together.

It's so important to have healthy ways to express what you are feeling, even if it means sharing your struggles, because it's a way of taking care of your mental well-being. I was fortunate that the right people came into my life during the pandemic when I was feeling at my worst. Without them, I wouldn't be here today sharing this with you.

If you're going through something right now, have the courage to take care of your mental well-being. It's okay to seek out professional help, and there's no shame in that. If you're on the journey to healing yourself, you do what works for you.

So many mental health resources are now available. Don't take it for granted. If it's available to you, take the opportunity to use it. Your future self will thank you for it.

2

The Challenges Asian Women Still Face

As an Asian woman, you face so many challenges in perception and mindset that hold you back from being considered for leadership roles. It's important to identify these challenges and name them so you find support or resources as you experience them. All women can relate to these challenges, no matter their culture.

The "Submissive" Stereotype

How many times have you heard Asian women described as quiet, submissive, and obedient? This negative stereotype hurts us as a whole because we are seen as an easy target to be bullied, attacked, and often not taken seriously.

If you're seen as quiet, submissive, and obedient, how can anyone see you as a leader? It's so important to dismantle the negative stereotypes that you and I face so that Asian women and all women can be seen as leaders.

The Hyper-sexualized Stereotype

Often, Asian women are seen as "exotic" and fetishized as sex objects. The hyper-sexualization of Asian women is dehumanizing, and a great example of that is the Atlanta shooting.

I remember when I first heard about the Atlanta spa shooting that took the lives of six Asian women. While the Asian community was in an uproar, the county sheriff mentioned that the shooter was having a "bad day" and that his "temptations" were the reasons why he decided to have a shooting spree in three different spa locations.[1]

Finally, when you thought that mainstream media was going to bring awareness to anti-Asian crimes that were happening, they were still talking about the shooter and not one mention of the victims. It took days before the media released the victims' names.

What's even worse was the fact that the victims of the Atlanta shooting were to blame for these senseless crimes because there were suspicions that they were sex workers and that led the shooter to kill them. Sex workers or not, there is no reason why any person should intentionally kill someone.[2]

I remember last year when a prime-time TV show in China asked me to be on a panel talking about the Stop Asian Hate Movement and the Atlanta Spa Shooting. One of the questions the host asked me was pertaining to the victims. He asked me if the victims being "alleged" sex workers was a major factor that contributed to their murders.

The recording of that segment is nowhere to be found, and part of me is a little bit relieved because I was totally nervous during that live interview. I do remember telling the host that just because the victims were seen as "alleged" sex workers, it doesn't give anyone the right to kill them. People are allowed to choose what they want to do; there is no judgment. Another thing

I mentioned is that many Asian women are also forced into this type of work. A person promises them that they will live the American dream and they are forced into prostitution to pay off a debt. So it's unfair to judge someone based on that notion.

How many times have Asian women been blamed for something that they didn't do? Why do Asian women constantly get crucified for situations when we are totally not in the wrong? Is this because of our upbringing, how society sees us, or both?

This hyper-sexualization can also affect your children. How many times have you heard of Asian girls and boys being sexually abused, trafficked, or forced into prostitution, especially in Asia? This is the sad truth that is never talked about. I come from a country where child trafficking is more common that you realize. I know that foreigners love visiting the Philippines not only for the sandy beaches but also because they can get away with breaking the law.

At one point, the age of sexual consent in the Philippines was 12 years old, but the country has raised it to 16 years old, which to me is still too young.[3] Here are other disturbing facts about human trafficking in the Philippines:

- The Philippines is one of the largest countries for sexually exploited children on the internet.
- About 50,000 children are domestic workers in the Philippines; almost 5,000 are under the age of 15.
- It's estimated that 60,000 to 100,000 Filipino children are victims of labor and sex trafficking.
- Human trafficking is the second largest criminal enterprise in the world, after narcotics.
- Most of the children who are victims of labor and sex trafficking are sold by their family members.[4]

This is just the facts of one country in Asia. Three countries in Asia are known as key destinations for human trafficking:

Cambodia, Laos, and Myanmar.[5] In fact, human trafficking victim support groups are urging the Association of Southeast Asian Nations (ASEAN) to step in and fight this prevalent problem.

Tens of thousands of Asians have been trafficked into Cambodia, Laos, and Myanmar for romance scams, video entrapment through video calls, secret recordings of lewd acts, credit card scams, phishing and copycat government websites, and fraudulent financial offers. Most of those being trafficked have been given false promises of high-paying jobs in towns that have a reputation for being lawless.

The Yellow Peril Stereotype

The dangers of hyper-sexualizing Asian women has had a long history, and it all started with the Yellow Peril, defined in this quote from the Student Digital Gallery at BGSU:

> *The term "Yellow Peril" refers to Western fears that Asians, in particular the Chinese, would invade their lands and disrupt Western values, such as democracy, Christianity, and technological innovation. However, ideas about Western progress at the time also included beliefs that are recognized as problematic today, such as white supremacy and the virtue of colonizing non-Western lands.*[6]

Because of the Yellow Peril, the United States and Canada passed laws that prohibited Asians from entering the country, such as the Chinese Exclusion Act. Asians were seen as a threat to the Western world and characterized as filthy and disease-ridden.

Asian women were perceived as prostitutes and accused of spreading sexually transmitted diseases at that time. This is where the negative stereotypes for Asian women began that still exist today.[7]

For centuries Asians have been a scapegoat for America, and today, Asian women face another form of Yellow Peril.

"Yellow Fever" Fetishization

Asian women have been fetishized for centuries. Most of the time, Asian women are seen as exotic and sexually submissive beings. Most non-Asian men think that Asian women are all about pleasing their man as the number one goal, that we'll do anything and everything for him. The term "Yellow Fever" has been used to describe this as well.

I remember one day I Googled the term "Asian women." The first articles that popped up were ones with titles like "How to Date an Asian Woman" or "Why Men Love Yellow Fever."

Even when I was looking for groups on Facebook on Asian women, most of the groups had something to do with dating:

- *Asian Women Looking for White Men*
- *Asian Women Looking for American Black Men*
- *Asian Women Meet Western Men*

The list goes on. It was appalling to think that Asian women were a prominent search for dating and matchmaking sites. Asian mail order bride sites have been popular with non-Asian men wanting to find the "quiet and submissive Asian wife" who will tend to their every need. This fetishization is hurtful and dehumanizing for Asian women.

Representation of Asian Women in Hollywood

Hollywood is also responsible for the challenges Asian women face. Typecasting of Asian actresses in TV and film has limited their roles to the maid, the prostitute, the geisha, the delicate flower, the submissive wife, or as the supporting and comic relief characters. Not only are these roles degrading, they perpetuate the hypersexualized view of Asian women.

At one point, NBC was about to give the green light to a TV show called *Mail Order Family*.[8] The premise was centered on a comedian woman whose father happens to have a Filipina mail order bride. There was major backlash from the Asian community when the show was announced. Having a TV show that shows Filipina women are nothing more than an object you can order off a catalog is totally inappropriate. People don't understand the traumas mail order brides go through. They've been forced into sex slavery, prostitution, and mental abuse. They are treated as if they are someone's property. In the end, NBC decided to cancel the show, but the question remains about the vetting process and how the storyline was deemed acceptable for a primetime TV show in the first place.

When you constantly see roles like these for Asian women, it's a slap on the face telling you that Asian women are not bankable enough to be their own lead in a movie or TV show. It reinforces the tendency of Asian women to feel invisible.

It was bad enough to lack Asian representation in Hollywood, especially when Asian characters were constantly replaced with white characters in the movies and TV. Remember when *Ghost in the Shell* came out? The movie was based on a Japanese anime, and the lead role went to Scarlett Johansson instead of using an Asian actress. The movie ended up bombing at the box office because the Asian American community was fed up.

I remember attending a virtual interview where Amy Tan was the guest of honor. She mentioned when *The Joy Luck Club* was slated to have a movie version, the production company initially planned to replace the characters with white people. Amy adamantly argued that the actors portraying the main characters had to be Asian. I am so glad she fought for that because *The Joy Luck Club* is one of my all-time favorite movies. It was the first movie I saw in Canada that had an all-Asian cast on the big screen.

One of my favorite movies that came out in 2022 was *Everything Everywhere All at Once*. I remember reading an interview with Michelle Yeoh and why she was so excited to be part of this movie:

> *This was the first time where I read this Asian immigrant woman [who] was the superhero in this movie. Evelyn Wang deserves her voice, to be heard—through the story that she must tell and the people that she loves in her world. Also what excited me was it encompassed so many different genres of film, and the only way they could really push this forward is [using] science fiction. In science fiction, you can really, really push the envelope to the stratosphere … so it's like there's almost like five genres of films in one movie. I get to do comedy, physical comedy, drama, romance, it's a love story.*[9]

The most invisible woman in the world, the immigrant Asian woman, has become the lead role and the heroine in the movie. How exciting is that? The Asian auntie whom you would see shopping at the Chinese grocery store minding her business and doing her own thing is now considered the heroine in the movie. An ordinary Asian woman became an extraordinary superhero, and that is what I love to see. I hope this will be the first of many Asian characters that you see in Hollywood.

The Representation of Asian Women in Mainstream Media

The representation of Asian women in mainstream media in general also affects how we are seen. Since the pandemic, Asians have been the scapegoat and have been targeted not only for hate crimes, but how the community is seen by mainstream media in general.

Every time a new COVID-19 variant emerged, news sites tend to use a photo of a masked Asian woman for the article. Time and time again you cry to mainstream media to stop doing this, but it keeps on happening.

I shared a post on LinkedIn about the *Chicago Sun-Times* and *New York Times* sharing a photo of a masked Asian woman in their article when the Omicron subvariant was on the rise. Representation like this inflames negative perceptions against Asians and makes Asian women even more vulnerable, especially when it comes to anti-Asian hate crimes.[10]

Two months later, I shared another post on LinkedIn where the *Washington Post* posted a photo of a masked Asian woman with the headline: "Coronavirus Wave This Fall Could Infect 100 million, Administrator Warns."[11]

Even the New York Department of Health and Mental Hygiene, when it tweeted about the latest Omicron variant in July 2022 included a photo of another masked Asian woman.[12] Incidents of violence against Asian women in New York, for example, had a huge uptick.[13] There are videos of Asian women lining up for hours on end just to buy a can of pepper spray. I had a conversation with an Asian lawyer in New York, and she mentioned how she used to feel safe even if she fell asleep in the subway on her way to work, but now she constantly checks her surroundings wherever she goes so that she doesn't become a target of a hate crime.

Even a 65-year-old Asian woman was attacked and robbed by two men in broad daylight on a Sunday morning while strolling in Queens.[14]

The day *Roe v. Wade* was overturned, I saw an article from the *Austin Chronicle* that had sponsored content promoting Asian mail order brides.[15] Even this "progressive" newspaper allowed content like this on their platform without a thought to how it perpetuates harm for Asian women. The media platforms don't understand the trauma an Asian woman goes through when she becomes a mail order bride.

There are many situations in which Asian women were treated as sex objects, forced into prostitution, and go through all kinds of abuse. Seeing that ad was the same as promoting human trafficking so long a it becomes a source of ad revenue.

I started sharing my frustrations and anger on social media. I called out people who had a bigger influence than me in the community to spread the message. The community was in an uproar because it was poor taste in the media to promote this kind of content on the same day women's rights were taken away.

The *Austin Chronicle* heard our message and took the ad out. They also published an apology and committed to prevent something like this from happening again. I started getting media attention on what happened, and it was great to see that people were aware of the kinds of situations that are harmful for Asian women.[16]

The *Austin Chronicle* was not the only publication responsible for promoting this kind of content online. Other media outlets like the *SF Weekly* and *East Bay Express* were running similar paid ads. Since then, they've been called out and have also taken down all their posts related to Asian mail order brides.

The *Washington City Paper* was another media platform that was promoting sponsored content harming Asian women with ads such as "Top Asian Cam Sites: The Best Asian Webcam Models and Online Cams."[17] Sometimes I wonder what the editorial process is like for media companies and how they allow this kind of content to be published. With the constant hypersexualization of Asian women that has been going on for centuries, this is the last thing you need in 2022.

Lack of Asian Women Leadership Representation in Other Industries

It's challenging to see yourself as a leader when you don't see other women who look like you as chief executive officers (CEOs) or in management and leadership positions. While some progress has been made, there's still a long way to go.

How many Asian women hold high positions in politics, sports, Fortune 500 companies, and other boardrooms? You'd be lucky to see one.

A study from Who Rules America shows the number of Asian women who held a CEO position in Fortune 500 companies from 2000–2020. Based on their data, only six Asian women were CEOs in Fortune 500 companies:

- Andrea Jung—CEO of Avon from 1999 to 2012
- Laura Sen—CEO of BJ's Wholesale Club from 2009 to 2012
- Lisa Su—CEO of Advanced Micro Devices from 2014 to present
- Joey Wat—CEO of Yuma China from 2018 to present
- Indra Nooyi—CEO of PepsiCo from 2006 to 2018
- Sonia Syngal—CEO of Gap Inc from 2020 to present[18]

In a span of 20 years, only six Asian women were able to become CEOs of Fortune 500 companies compared to 72 Caucasian women. That's a huge difference.

While more Asian women are in lower-level positions in companies, it's more challenging for you to move up the corporate ladder, and there are so many reasons why.

The negative stereotypes that you face is a main one. Most companies think Asian women are quiet and not assertive enough to be a leader. Other reasons are also mentioned:

- Having an Asian name that your peers cannot pronounce
- Not being able to speak English well because it's not your first language
- Having an accent

- Asian women are the least likely to get promoted
- Asian women are not seen as an underrepresented group due to the model minority myth

Studies have shown that Asian Americans have suffered from being promoted to management roles because of these reasons. A study from the University of Redlands mentioned that 28% of applicants with Asian names are less likely to get callbacks from potential employers, even if they have the same education and experience as the applicants with English names.[19]

The Pressure to Get Married

The Asian culture has programmed women that the number one goal is to get married. My aunts constantly ask me, "*When are you going to get married?*"

I have heard it all. I have been given prayer books so that I can pray for a husband. I was told I should go to church so that God can bless me with a husband. I would get all kinds of side eye when I tell people I was single, like I was a reject from society.

By my relative's standards, I am already considered an old maid, and there is a stigma when you are a single Asian woman in your 40s. You are seen in your culture as an outcast or that something is wrong with you because you are not married yet. Asia alone has many names for Asian women who are single at 25 years old and above.

In China, if you are 25 or over and still single, you are referred to as *Sheng-Nu*,[20] which literally means leftover. Never mind that these women are highly educated and have great career positions. If you are not married, you are a leftover; you are an embarrassment to your family and your culture.

In fact, every Valentine's Day in China, huge matchmaking parties are planned in the big cities in order to revive marriages since the numbers of marriages in China has dropped by half in the last 10 years.[21]

In Japan, they also have a term for Japanese women who are unmarried—*Christmas cake*—because after the holidays, nobody likes to eat Christmas cake, and you are referred to as unsold.[22]

In parts of Asia, arranged marriages are still prevalent today. Netflix even has a show called *Indian Matchmaking*, which is a reality show that follows a sought-out Indian woman matchmaker and follows her journey to help South Asian singles go through the process of arranged marriages. In 2022, arranged marriage is something that is unnecessary; there are so many ways to connect with a person or find your soulmate. The process of arranged marriages has been passed down from generation to generation, thinking it is the tradition when it's not.

A study from the World Population Review shared the ranking of arranged marriages in 2022 in Asia, and the top countries are India, China, Pakistan, Japan, Iran, Iraq, Indonesia, Bangladesh, and South Korea.[23]

An article from the online news outlet *Nextshark* talks about a Chinese woman who was admitted to the hospital due to severe anxiety after being constantly pressured by her parents to get married.[24] She was fed up with her parents constantly nagging her about getting married and got into a big fight with them. The woman started having panic attacks and other symptoms. She was later diagnosed with severe anxiety disorder.

Not only does it affect your mental health but it can also affect your physical health. I am sure this woman is not the only Asian woman who has been through a panic attack or worse because of Asian parents constantly begging their daughters to get married.

There is nothing wrong with getting married. I believe if you find the right person, then you should go ahead and get married, but the problem with the Asian culture is that most people marry for the wrong reasons. Most of the time, you get married so you are not an outcast from your culture, or you are told it is your duty to get married so you can make babies. Is that all you are good for?

The Need for Perfection

How many times have you been told to be the perfect daughter, wife, mother, sister, etc.? One time too many. All your life you had to always be perfect for everyone else. If you make a mistake, you feel like a failure to your family, peers, friends, culture, and society.

Perfection is an illusion, and it's unrealistic. It's impossible to achieve perfection in all aspects of your life because it doesn't exist.

All your life you have been pressured to be the best of everything, get straight As, go to the best universities, marry a man with status, and more. This pressure can get to you when you fail to meet the standards that are set by everyone else.

I wanted to remind you that nobody is perfect and that is okay. I am far from perfect, and for the longest time I thought I had to carry myself a certain way for others to like me or accept me as a person. I thought I always had to show up as the perfect Asian woman and feared of failure when I made a mistake.

I would always be jealous of other women whom I saw on social media and thought they had the perfect partner, life, and/or business.

What I didn't realize was that what you may see on social media is not what you see in real life. The photos that I saw may look perfect, but I never knew the struggles they were going through such as divorce, bankruptcy, abuse, and more.

When it comes to forging your own path or becoming an entrepreneur, all you constantly see is the success of others. You see all the glory but never hear the story. It's important to know that anyone's journey is never perfect, and that roadblocks, challenges, and mistakes will always be part of it because this is what will help you build the courage and confidence to keep moving forward. When you focus on trying to make everything perfect before you start, nothing ever gets done because you are still trying to perfect everything. I know this from experience many times.

Even when I decided to start my podcast, I delayed so many times because I thought everything had to be perfect to the tee. I kept waiting for the "perfect moment" to launch the podcast, and the longer I waited, the more time I was wasting. If it weren't for a friend who told me to put it out there, I wouldn't be here today.

I actually felt more at peace when I started interviewing so many Asian women on my podcast and realized that I wasn't the only person who was feeling pressure for the need to be perfect. The women on my podcast also had the same feelings as I did. There was a sense of relief knowing that I was not alone and that I could work through this.

The moment you realize that perfection isn't real, it will be easier for you to take the first step of your journey, move forward, and be the leader that you are meant to be.

Fear of Failure

Fear of failure is something that the Asian culture has ingrained in you from the moment you were born. Anything you do in life, you always have to be at the top of the game, and this can bring so much anxiety to you and your mental well-being.

In Asian culture, failure is never an option.

All my life I have always felt like a failure, and the first sign of failure started when I was a child. I didn't start talking until I was 5 years old. My parents thought there was something wrong with me because of it. They were relieved once I started talking, and now they tell me that I talk too much. I told them I had to make up for the 5 years that I didn't talk.

Even when I started school, I failed kindergarten in the Philippines for coloring outside the lines of a photo. For the whole school year, I could not get past this one photo to color within the lines. I kept coloring outside the lines of the photo to the point that the teacher gave me a new copy of the photo that I was supposed to color and still I colored outside the lines.

I failed kindergarten, moved to another school, and had to redo kindergarten all over again. I didn't realize how this one moment in my life always made me feel like I was a failure in all aspects of my life. I was constantly putting myself down and always thought the worst of me because of it.

Fear of failure is more common than you think. You see so many Asian students go to great lengths to get into the best schools so they can bring honor to the family name. If you fail to get into the best schools, you are seen as a failure in life and not accepted by society.

The pressure becomes so high that most students have a mental breakdown or a panic attack or, even worse, commit suicide. In fact, suicide is the leading cause of death for Asian Americans between the ages of 15 and 24.[25]

The Asian American Closet

Being an Asian woman is tough, but being a gay Asian woman is even tougher. I think one of the hardest things an Asian woman has to go through is to come out to her Asian parents about her sexual orientation. You have no idea what the outcome will be. You don't know if your Asian parents will accept you or disown you.

Not only do you have to fear the outcome of your Asian parents, you still have your Asian relatives, friends, and culture to deal with as well. Why is it so hard to come out to the ones you love the most? It's because the Asian culture has always lived one way that has been passed down from generation to generation, thinking that is the only way to live a successful life.

Anything outside of that is not accepted. That could be why it's so hard to be a gay Asian woman. You have to hide your identity and live a double life. It's exhausting, and you feel trapped because you can't live your true self.

A study from The Trevor Project, which created a National Survey on LGBTQ+ Youth (ages 13–24) reported that 38% of Asian/Pacific Islander youth considered suicide while 12% attempted suicide.[26]

A great example of this situation is my older sister. I love my sister with all my heart, and as a child, she always had crushes on girls. She never understood why she only liked girls, and she hid that part of her for a very long time. She always thought maybe something was wrong with her because she never had any attraction for boys.

My sister is in a loving relationship with her partner for over 20 years, and they have two beautiful daughters. Even though she has been in this relationship for so long, most of my relatives in the Philippines have no idea about this part of her life. In Canada, she is able to live as her true self, but when we go to the Philippines to visit my relatives, she has to hide her family and her identity.

My sister will be marrying my soon to be sister-in-law in the Philippines, which my parents are happily paying for. We are so excited to celebrate this wonderful occasion with her, but there are two special women in her life whom she would love to invite to her wedding but won't be able to. These two special women are my grandmothers.

My sister loves my grandmothers, and the feeling is mutual. She has always been the favorite of my grandmothers because she always makes sure to check on them. She calls them every week to see how they are doing, she sends them their favorite foods to eat, and even flies to the other side of the world once a year just to see them in person, even if it's for only one day. Every time my grandmothers see my sister on video chat, their faces just light up like they just won the lottery.

My sister loves my grandmothers with all her heart, and I know how heartbroken she is that she can never share this monumental celebration with them. We know that if my sister ever came out to my grandmothers, she would be disowned. My grandmothers are old school, and at their age, the last thing my sister wants is to give my grandmothers a heart attack if she ever decided to come out to them. Although my grandmothers can accept other people's children to come out of the closet, they cannot accept their own offspring coming out.

I have a huge family on my dad's side. My grandmother alone has 12 siblings. We have a huge family chat when we share what's going on with our lives and greet our relatives on their birthdays. One of my grandmother's nephews got married, and everyone in the family shared photos of the wedding.

My sister then saw my grandmother attend the wedding. This really broke her heart because this is something she really wants for her own wedding, and she knows deep inside her heart it will not be possible. My sister started crying when she saw pictures of my grandmother attending the wedding. She was depressed the whole day knowing something like this could never happen for her own wedding because she is marrying a woman.

This is a sad reality that most Asian women in the LGBTQ+ community face, and when I told my sister about writing this book, she actually wanted me to share her story here. She knows there are other Asian women out there who are going through a similar situation. My sister wants you to know that you are not alone in this journey.

In a speech that she delivered at her place of employment during Pride Month, my sister also shared her personal struggles: "*It's been really tough living an almost double life. Having to hide who I am and who my family is. Feeling like our love is less than because we are a same-sex couple. This is why Pride is so important; our love is not less than, we are not different. Love is love and that should be more than enough for the world to accept us.*"

The Beauty Standards of Asian Women

When it comes to beauty standards, Asian women are always seen as petite, thin-framed, and the most important, having pale white skin. You have been given another set of standards that is unattainable by any Asian woman.

Whitening products are a multibillion-dollar industry across the world. In 2020, it is reported that women of color spent $8.6 billion dollars on whitening products worldwide, and this amount is projected to increase to $12.3 billion by 2027.[27]

Having pale white skin was a sign of prestige and wealth in Asian culture. The more pale your skin is, the more you are accepted into society. In the country that I was born in, the Philippines, you see countless billboards of movie stars promoting all kinds of whitening products as a standard of beauty. Even traveling to other Asian countries such as Thailand and South Korea you also see big billboards promoting whitening products.

Asian women with darker skin were seen as not beautiful and were considered low class, which is far from the truth. I believe everyone should feel beautiful in their own skin regardless of the color of your skin.

There is always a competition when it comes to the standard of beauty. Everyone has the need to have the perfect face, the perfect frame, and the perfect body. I remember visiting

Gangnam during my stopover in South Korea; there is a plastic surgery office on every corner.

One of the most popular surgeries that many Asian women get is the double eyelid so that Asian women can look more Western.

Part of the reason why Asian women go through these beauty procedures is to assimilate to Western culture as well. Asian women want bigger eyes, a longer nose, and paler skin. These beauty standards become toxic for Asian women, which makes them feel like they are not enough.

This started back to the 15th century when Europeans considered Asian women as primitive and undesirable, which resulted in our culture obsessing over having a more European look.[28]

There's also the fat shaming that happens with Asian women. There's this misconception that all Asian women are size zeroes, when in reality Asian women come in many different sizes. I remember every time I would visit my aunts, the first thing they would say was, "*You got fat.*"

How many times have you received backhanded comments from your relatives that made you feel small because you didn't live up to a certain standard? Before, it would bother me so much, but when you start working on yourself, you learn to ignore the comments.

The world of social media doesn't help the standards of beauty as well. You see altered photos that paint the picture of the perfect face, body, and more. You have a distorted perception of what beauty is supposed to look like. It's even worse now that there are AI social media influencers who look too perfect and make you feel worse about yourself.

The standard of beauty is very toxic. It plays with your mind, and you think that you always have to do everything to achieve perfection. Even during the pandemic, there was a boom in the plastic surgery industry because people were suffering from Zoom dysmorphia. As people were stuck at home and having nonstop video Zoom meetings, they started to notice all the bad parts of themselves, whether it was saggy skin or a flat nose, and it led people to spend money to get it fixed even if it wasn't necessary.[29]

The Confidence Gap

One of the biggest things that women face from men is the confidence gap. Men are generally more confident than women. As a woman, even though you tend to over-prepare and be 110% ready for a presentation or a project, something still holds you back to push through. A man will just go for it even if he is 20% ready.

It's easier for a man to build confidence because he is not bogged down by the gender stereotypes you deal with. Every time a woman goes out and wants to be confident, she is already labeled as too much, too assertive, too aggressive, and too bossy, while a man takes the same actions, and he is praised for it.

It's even worse as an Asian woman because when you do something outside of the path you are told to live by, you're labeled as an outlaw or out of your senses. There are too many labels for a woman who forges her own path, and it hurts all women.

This confidence gap starts as early as the age of 8 for girls. A report from Ypulse shared some staggering information about girls' confidence. In the report they mentioned the following:

- Between ages 8 and 14, girls' confidence levels drop by 30%.
- Between tween and teen years, girl's confidence that other people like them goes from 71% to 38%, that's more than a 100% drop.
- More than half of teen girls feel pressured to be perfect.
- Three out of four teens worry about failing.

- Between ages 12 and 13, there is an increase of 150% who say that failure is not an option.
- Nearly 80% of girls want to feel more confident in themselves.[30]

It's alarming that girls as young as 8 years old are already dealing with confidence issues. No wonder women have such a huge confidence gap compared to men.

The Inequality Asian Women Face

As an Asian woman, you face so much inequality, and I am talking about just within the culture. Most of the time, your family will always favor the men over the women. Back in the day, if Asian parents could not afford to send all their kids to school, they would choose their sons over their daughters to finish school.

My grandmother had to quit school to take care of her siblings. She was able to make it to sixth grade before she had to leave.

Back in the day as an Asian woman, you have been told to never make any noise, do as you're told, and stay in the background. You are told to go school (if you are allowed to), get married, have kids, and run the household. You are only good for marriage and making babies.

In Chinese culture, if a woman gets married, it means that she is considered an outsider to her family and is now part of her husband's family. She cannot get any inheritance from her parents.

In parts of Asia, women also get treated unfairly.

In China, when a man and a woman get married and they own a home, the husband can have the ability to only name himself on the deed. This law, called the Marriage Law, gives men more power over women.[31] If a married couple decides to get a divorce, the man will get everything, while the woman is left with nothing.

I remember watching the movie called *Water*, which tells a story of an Indian girl in the 1940s whose husband passed away when she was 8 years old. Yes, you read that right. Child marriages is common in India. According to UNICEF, about 1.5 million Indian girls under the age of 18 get married in India.[32]

A widow in India is sent to a home where she is set to live her life as an outcast to society. This was a way for their families not to be financially responsible for them. During their time in the house, you can see the women being treated like dirt, and some were forced into prostitution. While the movie is based on a novel, widows in India still face harsh realities in the present day. It is said that India has around 55 million widows, who are called "vidhwa." The term "vidh" is a Sanskrit word meaning destitute.[33]

According to the Global Gender Index Gap report in 2022, which indicates the gap between men and women in political representation, economic empowerment, education, and health, the countries with the lowest rankings in Southeast and South Asia are Japan, Bhutan, and India.[34]

Japan is another country that does not value a woman's worth. Women in Japan still receive lower pay than men, and the representation of Japanese women in politics is scarce. While there are laws that promote having more women in politics, it is not enforced, which leads to fewer women running for office. Add the sexual harassment that women face while running in politics, and it becomes a turnoff for women to move forward.[35]

It's disheartening that we still face so many challenges as an Asian woman. It's no wonder why we resist from becoming the leader we are meant to be. We have so much unpacking to do especially with all the standards we have to live by from our family, our culture, and society.

Just remember, what people say about you is not your absolute truth; it's just someone's viewpoint. Don't ever let anyone dim your light. I remember a time when I wanted to look for a new job because I wanted something better for myself.

I started applying for new jobs, and when I told my male colleague, he asked me, "*Why would you look for another job when you make more than enough as a woman?*"

When he said that, I actually believed him, and for 12 years I was stuck at a job that I hated because I thought that was the best I can do. Imagine if I didn't believe his words. I would have been able to get a new job with new opportunities or started a business a lot sooner. But it's okay. Everything had to happen for a reason. That reason may be to share this story with you so that you can realize your own potential and not go through what I went through.

Now that you are aware of the challenges that Asian women face, it's time to move on and talk about intergenerational trauma, which is a topic that is hardly ever talked about in the Asian community. This is definitely an important topic that needs to be addressed separately. I do a deep dive into the topic in the next chapter.

3

Intergenerational Trauma and Why We Need to Talk About It

THE TRAUMAS YOU carry are passed on from the historical trauma that your parents, grandparents, and ancestors also bore. A woman I met at a networking event told me that the traumas can go four generations deep. That is a big opportunity for self-awareness that helps you move forward as a leader. In fact, this is one of the most important parts of your journey.

Jeanie Chang, who is a licensed family and marriage therapist and the creator of Noona's Noonchi, defines intergenerational trauma as: "*...the trauma that gets passed down from those who directly experience it to the following generations. The trauma begins with an incident or event that affects an individual or multiple family members*."[1]

All your life, as an Asian woman:

- You were told to be the perfect daughter, wife, sister, mother, colleague, and friend.
- You are constantly compared to other people in your circle of influence, whether it's family or friends.

- You have been told countless times to always take care of everyone else.
- You are told to never share the traumas that you went through but to keep them to yourself.
- You are told to never share how you are feeling.
- You are told to never share your opinions.
- When something traumatic does happen, you are blamed for it, even if it's not your fault.
- You are constantly seeking approval from your parents, peers, and people of higher influence.
- You have been forced to do something that you did not want to do because you wanted to save face or not tarnish the family name.
- You have been belittled for every mistake you have made.
- You were pressured to marry someone just for the sake of being married and not being seen as an outcast.
- You have been seen and treated as a sex object.
- You were constantly pressured to have the best grades in school; you must have the perfect score or straight As to be deemed worthy.
- You are constantly pleasing others.
- You have been told countless times how to live your life, which is to go to school, get a job, get married, never rock the boat, and be in the background.

This has been passed on from generation to generation, thinking that this is the "successful" way to live even though this has been hurting Asian women for centuries. If you keep on doing the same thing over and over, thinking this is the only way to live, how are you supposed to be open to new opportunities in your own life?

Of course, this is something that is never talked about in our culture because we have been conditioned for so long to never ever share what we are going through, and that is why so many

Asian women are hurting, feeling like we are invisible, and our voice doesn't matter. This makes us an easy target of anti-Asian hate crimes because no matter what happens, our ancestors have endured worse in their lifetimes, and if they didn't complain, then why should we complain about our own traumas.

The intergenerational traumas that you carry goes as far back in history and have been passed on from generation to generation. It will take a lot to unpack this type of trauma, but you have to start somewhere.

How Intergenerational Trauma Shows Up for Asian Women

Intergenerational trauma can show up in so many ways, and there are different situations and experiences for each person.

In my own family, my grandmother has had her fair share of traumatic experiences in her life that she will never tell a soul because that's what she has been told to do all her life. Every time you ask her about her life, she just shuts down, ignores the question, or changes the subject. It's unfortunate that our family will never know, and I want to know so that I can help her heal through her own journey.

I realized that I was the same way before I started to work on myself. I would never share what I was going through. I would shut down when my family would confront me with a situation, or I would just avoid the subject. I didn't realize that this all stemmed from my grandmother, because she did the same thing. I'm sure she learned this from my ancestors because she was taught to do the same thing.

I mentioned that intergenerational trauma can go as deep as four generations back, but for Asian women, it goes way deeper than you expected, and this is why you go through so many self-esteem and mental health issues.

Some Asian women experience a great deal of intergenerational trauma. There have been instances where women get constantly abused physically, sexually, and mentally, which can take a toll on a person's overall well-being.

I have spoken to Asian women who have been molested by their male peers whether it was their parent, uncle, friends, or even sibling and was just told to keep it quiet because you never want to air your dirty laundry out. You keep the skeletons in the closet, and you just constantly endure the abuse because that is what you have been told to do. It's now normalizing the situation because you think this is the only way you are supposed to live your life. When you have a daughter of your own and she is going through a similar situation, you tell her the same thing, which is to keep quiet and just endure it for the sake of saving face.

A study from the DC Coalition to End Domestic Violence[2] mentions the staggering statistics of violence against Asian and Pacific Islander American women during Sexual Assault Awareness Month in 2022. Here's the summary of their report:

- The Centers for Disease Control and Prevention (CDC) reported that 18% of Asian and Pacific Islander American women reported that they have experienced rape, stalking, and/or physical violence by an intimate partner.
- The Asian Pacific Institute on Gender-Based Violence reported that 68% of Filipinas and 50% of Indian and Pakistani women admitted to being sexually abused by an intimate partner.
- According to a study of 27 universities in America, 13% of Asian women reported experiencing nonconsensual sexual contact involving physical force or incapacitation compared to 3% of Asian males and 2% of Asian transgender, gender queer, gender nonconforming, questioning, or not identified individuals.

- The main reasons why Asian women survivors of sexual abuse don't talk about their experience were because 67% thought it would affect their reputation, 45% did not want to ruin the family's reputation, 42% were afraid of potential victim blaming, 37% were afraid of being isolated from friends and society, and 33% were afraid of a possible retaliation from their abuser.
- According to the National Organization of Asians and Pacific Islanders Ending Sexual Violence: "*Sexual assault is an issue that is discussed less by Asian Pacific Islanders since it is perceived to be connected to sexuality, a taboo subject, rather than a power issue. As such, estimates of rape among Asian and Pacific Islander women are likely too low as they are least likely to report sexual assault for reasons of 'language, culture, and mistrust of law enforcement.'*"

If these statistics are what were reported, imagine how many more unreported cases have happened and are still happening. In fact the number of sexually abused cases has significantly increased during the pandemic with the forced lockdowns and easier access to the internet.[3]

These stats are likely much higher due to our cultural upbringing. Many Asian women still endure in silence, thinking this is how life works.

The Centuries of Intergenerational Trauma for Asian Women

Not only do Asian women face intergenerational trauma but they also experience a history of traumas that have been passed on for centuries. There will be many history timelines from different parts of the world because it's important to show how deep the traumas of Asian women go. If you don't talk about where it took place and the situations that led to where you are today, nothing will ever get better.

China's cultural practices in marriage have affected Asian women in the way they've been treated and valued throughout history. China has had a long history of treating Asian women as objects. From forced marriages to having multiple wives, a Chinese woman was only good for getting married and birthing babies. Anything beyond that was not acceptable because it didn't fit in the path that was determined by our ancestors. There are many other reasons for marriage, such as if a woman was from a lower class, she was arranged to be married off to a wealthier family to have a better life. Another reason was binding two powerful families as one for business purposes. There are several ancient Chinese marriage traditions that I think are important to go through:

Nüwa and Fu Xi's fabled marriage (2600 BCE). These characters from Chinese mythology were responsible for creating mankind. They were both related by blood and started the tradition of marriage by being able to marry each other. This led to sibling marriages being allowed in China.

Neolithic Age. Toward the end of this era, China decided to ban sibling marriages but allowed to have maternal marriages where the son-in-law would live with his wife's family and was not allowed to have multiple wives at the same time.

Zhou Dynasty (1046–221 BCE). Sororate marriage was introduced where a man is allowed to marry his wife's sister or cousin if she is alive or dead.

Han Dynasty (206 bce–220 CE). This was the introduction of the exchange of betrothal gifts, from the groom's family to the bride's family, and the dowry, which came from the bride's family. The betrothal gifts was an important factor in a marriage because it represented honor. Once the exchange was made, the bride would be living in the groom's ancestral home for the rest of her life even if her husband passed away before her.

If a bride wanted to remarry after her husband's death, the bride's family would have to pay a certain amount to the deceased husband's family in order to get her back. Also, it was during this dynasty that marriage brokers or matchmakers were introduced, when elder Asian ladies would match couples to marry.

Qing Dynasty (1644 to 1912). Polygamy was introduced at the end of this dynasty for the sole purpose of fathering heirs. It was important to have a son in Chinese culture in order to keep the patriarchal lineage. If a man couldn't bear a son with his first wife, he would have multiple wives to increase his chances of having a son.[4]

Also introduced in this dynasty was concubines. If a woman was a concubine, she was not legally or socially married. She was only recognized as a sexual partner, expected to have children, and could be divorced at any time. The status of a concubine was improved in the latter part of the Qing Dynasty where a concubine can be promoted to wife if she was the mother of the only surviving sons.

Additionally, oppressive rituals became part of the marriage custom, such as feet binding. It was a way to amplify the beauty of a woman's foot, which offered a greater chance for a girl to get married and was seen as a girl's high social status. In 1912, the practice of feet binding was finally ended by the Chinese government.

In Korea, women had the freedom to mingle with men, have possession, and even inherit land during the Goryeo Dynasty. That soon changed after the Imjin War during the second half of the Joseon Dynasty.[5]

During the Joseon Dynasty, Korean women went expected to follow stricter rules. Women were to be virtuous, modest, obedient, and faithful. Women became a subordinate to their male relations. For a child, they had to obey their father. For married women, they had to obey their husbands. For elderly women, they would obey their sons.

In this dynasty, women had no right to inherit anything since their families had to pay an expensive dowry when they got married. Once a woman was married, she had to obey her husband's in-laws and had no right to ask for a divorce. Since she was considered to be in the husband's family, the bride's family didn't feel the need to leave any inheritance for her.

Even though the married women were not allowed to ask for a divorce, the men had the right to divorce their wife based on "the seven sins":

- Disobedience toward in-laws
- Inability to bear a son
- Adultery
- Jealousy
- Hereditary diseases
- Talkativeness
- Theft

If I were a bride at that time, I'm sure my husband would have divorced me right away for being too talkative. Isn't that the silliest reason for a man to divorce a woman? But that's how it was during that period.

If you became a widow, you were not allowed to remarry unless you married someone with lower class since it was often ignored. Men, however, could have multiple wives and concubines. I mean, how unfair and unjust is this?

In India, history has also shown us that Indian women were treated unfairly. An article written by Brenda Koushik shares about the "5 Old Indian Customs That Denied Women Human Rights."[6] The purpose of her article was to be a voice for Indian women who went through so much suffering dating back 400 CE. These are the customs that she shared in her article:

1. **Sati or Suttee.** Since men were considered an object for worship for Indian women, if the husband died and she became a widow, it meant her life was over. Back in the day, the dead husbands' bodies were burned using firewood, and the widow would have to be burned alive with the dead even if she didn't consent. But if the wife died, the husband was free to remarry another woman. The practice of burning the widow to death with her dead husband was a sign that she would have a place in heaven and would not live life in sin or disgrace as a single woman. The practice went on for years, and the last one was performed in 1987 when an 18-year-old girl was sacrificed in this ritual. The government created the Sati Prevention Act to punish people who still practice sati.
2. **Periods and Untouchability.** When a woman was menstruating, she was forced to live in a tiny hut outside her home for 5 days because she was considered impure. It was even considered a sin if people looked at her during the 5 days of menstruation. There were so many restrictions for women during their period, such as they were not allowed to touch anyone or anything, and they were not allowed to attend religious ceremonies, temples, or any festivals. When an Indian woman gets her period for the first time, it was a celebration for her. They would prepare a big ceremony because it was a sign that she was ready to get married. This is why periods have been such a taboo to speak about in any culture. What is natural for a woman is considered to be dirty and impure.
3. **Child Marriages and Widowhood.** Child marriages still exist today, and Indian girls as young as 10 to 12 years of

age are sold off by their family to marry men who can be old enough to be their grandfather. Indian girls were never sent to school and received no education. Instead they did chores outside of their home as a sign that they were unmarried and ready to make the union. Also, there was the practice of cradle marriage, when parents have already picked a spouse for their newborn baby. If the newborn baby girl's husband-to-be dies, she is already considered a widow with no chance of re-marriage. This is just appalling. It's bad enough that a husband is already chosen for them once they come out into world but to be labeled a widow and an outcast is just too cruel for words. Also women and girls who became widows were forced to live a stern and plain life and were not allowed to remarry ever, just like in the movie *Water*, which is based on this widowhood in India. Widows had to wear a plain white saree as a sign of honor for her husband's family. Even though a "Widow Remarriage Act" was passed in 1856, widows not being allowed to remarry still continued.

4. **Devadasis.** After reading what Devadasis is, I was appalled. It was the practice of giving young unmarried Indian girls to temples to be considered a slave of that god. Girls who were 8 to 12 years of age were given to the temple and were sexually abused by rich men and the temple priest. The practice dates back to as early as the ninth century. In certain villages, poor families who could not afford to care for their daughters and gave them away, thinking it was part of their calling to be sent away to be Devadasis. The practice has been banned since the 1940s. It's really disgusting when men decide to use religion as an excuse to sexually abuse a child. They don't understand the trauma she goes through and how that gets passed onto the next generation.

5. **Dowry Harassment and Female Infanticide.** Dowry is prevalent in most Asian countries, and India is part of this process as well. The bride's family would give some form of payment to the husband's family, whether it was money, land, jewels, gold, or the equivalent of these possessions. If the bride's family was not able to pay the dowry, they were harassed, threatened, and would suffer the consequences at the hand of the husband's family. This is why so many Indian girls were not able to go to school. From the moment they were born, the parents saved as much money as possible to pay a dowry, so sending their daughters to school would be a waste of their finances. Also Indian sons were favored over Indian daughters because they were preserving the family lineage. Because of this, many unborn baby girls were killed inside the womb or newborn girls were killed or abandoned after birth.

Other things that Indian women have been enduring for years are acid throwing, honor killings, and being accused of witchcraft.

In America, there is a long history of Asian women being treated unfairly, resulting in generations of intergenerational trauma or historical trauma. The problem was that nobody ever talked about this because it was also never taught in schools.

One of these historical facts was the Page Act of 1875, a law that prohibited Chinese women from entering the country because they were seen as prostitutes and were considered a threat to the morality of America. In 1882, The Chinese Exclusion Act also banned Chinese men and most people from Asia from entering the country.[7]

About the same time, Chinese women living in San Francisco were blamed by white men who got sexually transmitted diseases and was passed on to their wives.[8]

In 1899, British novelist and poet Rudyard Kipling wrote a poem called *The White Man's Burden: The United States and The Philippine Islands*, which encouraged Europeans to take control of the Philippines and its people; it was written at the time of the Philippine-American war. In the poem, he described Filipinos as "Half devil and half child."[9]

The Filipino-American War killed about 200,000 Filipino civilians. An article from *Harper's Bazaar* talks about the brutality Filipinas went through during this time and after.

Countless records showcase the brutalities endured by Filipina women because of the US military, which led to incarcerations, forced labor, sexual coercion, and more. In the article, Genevieve Clutario shared what Filipina women had to endure:

> *They faced forced prostitution, rape, and the abandonment of mixed-race children. While America would hold formal control over the Philippines until 1946, these systems of sexual coercion continued long after as part of official U.S. policy, until at least 1991.*[10]

In the same article, the Eighth Army, working in Japan, introduced a new program called R&R, or rest and recuperation, in 1950. What started as a way for American soldiers to step away from the loneliness, exhaustion, and dangers of their job soon became a comfort station for soldiers where they exploited Asian women for their pleasure. The term R&R was soon known as "rock and ruin," "rape and run," and "rape and restitution." These comfort stations spread to other countries in Asia such as Korea, Vietnam, Taiwan, Okinawa, Philippines, Vietnam, Thailand, Malaysia, Singapore, and others.

This also stems from the Imperial Japanese Army introducing the practice of using comfort women from 1932–1945. The term "comfort women" originated from the Japanese word "ianfu" which meant "comforting consoling women."

Women and children from different parts of Asia were kidnapped and forced into sex slavery to appease the soldiers' sexual appetites. The purpose of comfort stations and comfort women was to reduce the number of rapes and diseases that was happening during that time. Being able to have these comfort stations was a way to control it, but the turnout was worse. Most of the women that were affected were as young as 14 years old.

If the women were not kidnapped, they were purchased from families as legal servants, and while they spanned all over Asia, the three countries that were most affected were Korea, China, and the Philippines. Based on the data researched, they claimed that about 200,000 women were forced into being comfort women, but many women were undocumented so that number is likely way higher.

After comfort stations were abolished, many of the comfort women felt shame to go back home because of what had happened to them. Some women were raped every single minute. Many of these women became societal outcasts because of it and died from sexually transmitted diseases, suicide, or violent actions from Japanese soldiers. For the longest time, the Japanese erased any history that had to do with comfort stations and comfort women, stating it never existed. As the victims started to share their stories and the horror they went through, the Japanese could not hide from it anymore.[11]

I watched a Korean movie called *I Can Speak*. The movie centers on an old Korean woman who frequently visits the district office to complain and sees one of the workers who can speak fluent English. She then approaches the man to teach her how to speak English, and they go on this journey where the man teaches the old woman how to speak English. The sole purpose of the old woman learning to speak English was so she could travel to the United States to speak up about the horrific events that happened to her and her best friend when they were comfort women during the war. This movie is such a tearjerker. I think I finished a whole box of Kleenex when the old woman started speaking up about her experience as a comfort woman and how much she suffered from it.

All of this stems from the hyper-sexualization of Asian women and the negative stereotypes we face as being quiet, submissive, and obedient. Asian women are seen as the exotic beings that men can just treat as objects, and we will never complain because of the model minority myth. This is intergenerational trauma that we may have experienced since the beginning of time, but nobody ever talks about it.

Have you noticed that countries in Asia always wanted to protect the familial lineage? It was always important to bear a son to carry the family name and the only way to do that was to have multiple wives or concubines bear a son. In most of the countries in Asia, Asian women were always told what to do for the sake of their families and their culture. All these traditions never benefited Asian women; they always benefited Asian men and men in different countries like the United States. If this is all you ever knew as a woman and it was constantly passed down from generation to generation, how can you expect the change you want to see if you are not aware of the past things our ancestors have done to create so much trauma for you?

Knowing this, I realized how much unpacking I had to do to move forward in my own journey because this is not only trauma that I carry from my ancestors, but it's trauma that comes from my culture, which is centuries of making women feel small. I hope this history lesson can help you realize the traumas that you have to unpack so that you can move forward.

Hollywood Representation Tackling Intergenerational Trauma

Since there has been more Asian representation in Hollywood, I wanted to share three of my favorite movies that explore different scenarios of intergenerational trauma with Asian women.

Turning Red

When I first saw the trailer for this movie, I had no clue what it was about, but I was excited because it had an Asian girl as the lead character and it was set in Toronto. Just those two things sold me on watching the movie.

When I watched it for the first time on Disney+, I just loved it even more not only because of the story but also the many parts of Toronto, my beloved city, that I got to see. You got to see the TTC (Toronto Transit Commission), which is our public transit system, and the CN Tower, and even our beloved Tim Hortons made the cut.

This movie was a movie that every Asian kid can relate to. In the beginning of the movie you can already relate to it when the lead character, Meilin Lee or Mei, who is a 13-year-old Chinese Canadian girl, strives to be the perfect daughter to her parents. In the opening scene, Mei says:

> *The number one rule in my family…* HONOR YOUR PARENTS! *They are the supreme beings who gave you life, who sweated and sacrifice so much to put a roof over your head, food on your plate, an* EPIC *amount of food. The least you can do in return, is….* EVERY SINGLE THING THEY ASK!

How many times in your life as an Asian woman do you hear that number one rule from your Asian parents? Your parents gave you life and sacrificed everything to give you a better life. This is all they ask in return, to do everything else they tell you. This is another line in the movie in the opening scene that Mei said:

> *Of course some people are like... BE CAREFUL! Honoring your parents sounds great but if you take it too far, well, you might forget to honor yourself!*

Isn't that always the case? You do so much to honor your parents because that's what you have been told all your life. It's the golden rule. You honor them so much that you forget to honor the most important person, which is yourself.

I am not saying you should not honor your parents. I love my parents and everything they have done for me, but I also had to realize that I had to forge my own path even if they didn't understand it at the time. We had our arguments and disagreements of how I should live my life, but I always knew I wanted more.

I remember when I quit my job, my father was livid! He got so mad at me and started screaming as to why I decided to quit my job when I was already successful. His definition of success was not my definition of success, and he didn't understand that at the time. Most Asian parents, when they migrate to the United States or Canada, they just want their kids to go to a good school, get a good paying job, and work there until they retire.

That is not how I wanted to live my life, not that working for a job is a bad thing. If you love your job, that is great. I always say do what you love and create your own definition of success. Deep inside, I knew working a 9-to-5 job wasn't for me.

I can relate to Mei's character. When she was with her friends, she gets to be herself, but the moment she is with her mother, Ming, she becomes the perfect daughter who does no wrong.

She does everything she can to please her mother so she throws her friends under the bus, hides the fact that she has a crush on a boy, and that her favorite boy band is 4 Town, which her mother considers filth. Her mother also disapproves of the group of friends Mei hangs out with. The last thing Mei wants to do is to disappoint her mother.

As a good Asian daughter, you always want to seek approval from your parents, myself included. If I felt like if I didn't get their approval, I thought I was a total failure as a daughter. For years, I would always do what my parents told me to do. I always wanted to make sure I was the good daughter and that every decision I made I had to ask for their permission to make sure it was the right decision.

I remember when I bought a car without my dad's permission. He was furious with me because he wasn't there at all during the decision and buying process. You see, my dad loves cars and always wants to be part of anything that has to do with cars, whether there's something that needs to be fixed or if we plan to buy one. My very first car, my dad was the one who found it for me. So when I told him that I bought another car, he freaked out, asking me why I didn't tell him about it.

When I brought the car to the house, he checked every part of the car and told me every single thing that was wrong with it. He told me the mileage was too high, there was a scratch somewhere, and a crack on the front window. At that moment, I thought I made the worst decision of my life because my dad did not approve of the car that I bought.

When I was telling my ex-boyfriend about the car situation with my dad, he actually praised me because it was the first decision that I made all by myself without asking my parents' permission. Whether it was a good or bad decision, the most important part was that *I* made the decision. That was a huge wake-up call for me because it was the first time I realized that I can make my own decisions without constantly having to ask for others' opinions or permission.

And to be honest, the car I bought wasn't bad at all. Yes, the mileage was higher than the average, but it ran really well and hardly had any problems with it. Even my mechanic told me it was a good car.

Throughout *Turning Red*, you see Mei's red panda coming out when she learns to be her true self, talks about getting her period and going through puberty for the first time, which is often a taboo in our culture. At first, Mei doesn't really know how to handle her red panda, but as she keeps embracing it, her true self starts to come out more. It also helps that she has a great set of friends who are in this journey with her. The more Mei starts to bring her true self out, Ming starts to think she is losing her perfect daughter and starts to control her every move.

Ming went through the same situation as Mei by also being the perfect daughter to her own mother, Wu. When Ming's red panda came out, her mother controlled the situation and made sure it never came out again. Ming also went through the same situation as Mei growing up doing everything she can to please her own mother, Wu.

There is even a scene in the movie where the phone rings and Ming's husband tells her that it's her mom on the phone. She quickly hides and tells her husband that she's unavailable. When Ming's husband gives her the phone, you can see how nervous she is to talk to her own mother.

When Wu and her friends decide to visit Ming and Mei to fix the situation, you can see how Wu tries to control Ming. She judges Ming for her every move and blames her for Mei not acting appropriately.

Toward the end of the scene where Mei's red panda and Ming's red panda come face-to-face, it's the first time Mei tells her mother she's tired of being the perfect daughter. Mei even starts to gyrate in front of Ming as a way of rebelling back. This made Ming furious because all she ever wanted for Mei was to be the perfect daughter just like herself.

The movie takes you into another scene where Mei sees a teenage version of Ming crying because she felt like a failure not being the perfect daughter to Wu. In that moment, Mei consoled her mother saying she was a great mother, and she wasn't a failure. Ming also realized that her daughter was growing up and that she had to let her go to become her own person.

In the end, you see Ming accepting Mei more as her own person. She accepts Mei's friends and gives her enough freedom to find herself as a teenager. Although a part of Ming misses the times she had with her daughter, she understands that this is what she has to do.

I also love the last quote in the movie where Mei says:

> *We've all got an inner beast. We've all got a messy, loud, weird, part of ourselves hidden away, and a lot of us never let it out, but I did. How about you?*

I know how tough it can be trying to figure out who you truly are especially in a culture that tells you to live and be a certain way. In *Turning Red*, you see Mei wrestle with being able to come out as her true self or hide her identity to please her mother. Even Mei's mother, Ming, went through the same thing as a child. She also had to be the perfect daughter for her mother. Ming raised Mei the way she only knew how, the same way her mother raised her. This is a cycle that keeps happening from generation to generation because that is all our parents, grandparents, and ancestors ever knew. When you are aware of this then it's up to you to break the cycle and find a way to heal like how Mei and her mother were able to do in the movie.

Umma

I'm a huge fan of Sandra Oh, a phenomenal Canadian actress and a huge advocate for the community. If there's a movie that she's in, I'm there to watch it. This was also one of the reasons why I was excited to watch *Red Panda.* When I saw the trailer for *Umma,* it was definitely a movie that I was waiting to watch. *Umma* is the Korean word for mother, and the movie centers around a single mother, Amanda, and her daughter, Chrissy, who live on an isolated bee-keeping farm. Amanda's worst fear was that she was going to turn into her mother that she has been hiding from for years.

That fear came to fruition when Amanda's uncle from Korea suddenly arrived at her home. The uncle told Amanda how he wanted to bring over her dead mother's ashes since she passed away. He also told her it was Amanda's responsibility to give her mother a proper burial.

Amanda wanted nothing to do with her mother. In the opening scene, you hear a child, who happens to be Amanda, pleading and screaming to let her out of the locked room. Fast forward to Amanda's adult life; she totally lives off the grid with her daughter, Chrissy. Unlike her relationship with her Umma, Amanda seems to have a very close relationship with her daughter, but you know something is off. Amanda has no electronic devices or any kind of electricity in the house and tells her daughter that she gets sick if electricity is near her. You also see Amanda go through moments of her own PTSD from the trauma she had with her mother, such as seeing a silhouette of her Umma along with hearing lightning. Chrissy goes over to console her when she has her moments of PTSD.

Chrissy also lives an isolated life with no friends other than her mother and the man who buys their honey supply, named Danny. Amanda also home-schools her daughter, which is why she has no friends. In the movie, Chrissy starts a friendship with Danny's niece.

When the ashes of Amanda's mother are left at her farm, strange things start to happen. At the same time, her daughter Chrissy wants a life outside of the farm where she can be her own person. One of the things she wanted to do was to go to college. Amanda finds out about Chrissy's college application and is not happy about it because it feels like history is repeating itself. Chrissy is going to leave Amanda for a new life just like what she did to her Umma.

This movie is more of a supernatural twist since Umma's spirit makes many attempts to take over Amanda's body and strange things start to happen in the house, which could also be interpreted as part of Amanda's PTSD from the abuse she received from her mother as a child. In the movie, you also see a pattern of Amanda sheltering Chrissy from the world and being the overbearing Asian mother. She doesn't want to let Chrissy go just like how Umma did not want to let Amanda go.

In one scene, Amanda talks to Chrissy about her grandma, which Chrissy never knew about. Amanda shows her the things that were left in the suitcase that she wanted to take in the afterlife and also left for her burial ceremony. Amanda mentions that some Koreans believe that life's hardships are caused by the tormented spirits of their ancestors and make offerings to appease their tortured souls. This was a superstition that Amanda doesn't believe in, but I thought it was important to include since we are talking about intergenerational trauma and how this can affect your hardships in some way.

In the movie you learn that Amanda's mother was angry with life because before she got married, she was a dressmaker. Umma loved being a dressmaker, but she had to give that up when she got married. Umma had to leave the profession she loved and be the dutiful wife to her husband and travel to America for a better life.

Umma struggled a lot when she moved to America because everything was new to her. She got scared and never left the house. Amanda's dad eventually left her and Umma because he couldn't accept how Umma changed so much from when they met.

Because of that, Umma had a lot of pent-up anger, rage, and regret that she had to raise Amanda on her own. Umma took the anger, rage, and resentment out on Amanda by electrocuting her with a wire of an electric lamp that she broke and locking her in a closet. This is why electricity of any kind wasn't allowed in Amanda's house.

Also, the main reason why Umma haunts Amanda is because she is angry at Amanda for running away and leaving her to die on her own. In the movie, you see Amanda and Umma make peace with each other, and Umma is able to move on. Amanda also realizes that what Umma did to her is the same pattern she is following with Chrissy. She knews that she has to let Chrissy go and live her life.

In the last scene, Amanda and Chrissy give Umma a proper burial ceremony to make peace. Chrissy now owns a cellphone, and Amanda helps her pack for college. You can tell they are able to heal from the traumas they experienced and now have a better relationship with each other. Even though it's tough for Amanda to let Chrissy go, she knows that it was time for Chrissy to find her true self as well.

As Asian women, we always have to be the person to let go of our dreams in order to make the other person happy. In the case of Umma, she gave up her dream of being a passionate dressmaker in order to be the dutiful wife, and she never expressed her feelings about it. Instead she took her anger out on Amanda. Amanda also took out her frustrations with her own mother on Chrissy.

Keeping in your anger and resentment never helps because you end up hurting the person you love the most, and it becomes a cycle that's passed on again from generation to generation.

The Joy Luck Club

The Joy Luck Club is the first movie I saw with an all-Asian cast. It was the first time I saw true Asian representation in Hollywood. I can watch this movie over and over again. I just love this movie and the totally relatable stories they share about to our culture and the way Asian girls were brought up in the Western world.

The movie centers on the conflict over cultural values and complicated relationships among four first-generation Chinese American women and their mothers. I will do my best to explain the mother-daughter relationship for each set: Suyuan and June, Lindo and Waverly, Ying-Ying and Lena, and An-Mei and Rose.

Suyuan and June

The movie starts with the story of June (who narrates most of the movie) and her mother, Suyuan. June starts with this line in the movie:

> *When I was nine years old, my mother's version of believing in me was believing that I could be anything, anything she wanted, the best piano prodigy this side of China.*

June hated the piano and never practiced, but she was fortunate enough that her piano teacher was deaf at the time. When it was time for June's piano recital, it turned out bad because she didn't play the notes right. Suyuan was angry that June embarrassed her in front of the whole school including her friends. She made June turn off the TV and practice the piano, which she refused. Suyuan told June:

> *There two kinds of daughters: obedient or follow own mind. Only one kind daughter could live in this house, obedient kind.*

June responded back wishing she wasn't Suyuan's daughter and that she was dead like her twin half-sisters in China. June never understood why her mother left her twin half-sisters to die, and Suyuan never spoke about it, which made matters worse. June was furious that her mother left her twin daughters to die in China not knowing the real reason. This is typical in the older generation. They never talk about the hardships and traumas they went through and always keep it to themselves.

In another scene in the movie when Suyuan was still alive, and she serves dinner to the gang. Everyone loved her crab dish and reminds June that she made the best dish. To June, she believed that her mother always wanted to have the best including herself, but June felt like she was the biggest disappointment to her mother. During the dinner conversation, her friend Waverly tells June that the copy she wrote for their big firm was denied. As much as June wanted to fix it, Waverly told her that it wasn't sophisticated enough to be accepted. June was hurt, of course, that her work was rejected by Waverly's firm. It was even worse when Suyuan said that June's style is unlike Waverly's.

After the dinner party, June and Suyuan were cleaning up, and June starts the conversation saying how she is such a disappointment to her mother in every way because she is not like Waverly. Suyuan tells June she never expected anything from her but only hopes for the best for June. For June, even hope was a bad thing because it still felt like an expectation, and if she didn't meet it, she still saw herself as a disappointment.

Suyuan opens up to June saying that she sees June for who she really is, someone who has the best-quality heart. She goes on to tell June that she has style that cannot be taught and repeats to June that she truly sees her.

June prepares for her trip to China to meet her long-lost twin sisters who are still alive. Her father gives her a set of photos of Suyuan in China as a gift to the twin sisters. Then he starts to tell the story of why Suyuan had left the twins in China. This happened during a time when the Japanese took over China and everyone was running away from the chaos that was happening. You see Suyuan pushing a wheelbarrow with her twin girls inside. Suyuan was getting weaker and with no medicine available to make her feel better, she didn't know if she would be able to save herself and her children. Suyuan begged for people to take her babies so they could have a better life, but nobody paid attention to her. She left her babies by the tree with everything she owned including a photo of her and a note saying to bring the children to their father because she didn't want to die next to her children. She thought dying next to them would bring the babies bad luck.

Instead of dying, Suyuan woke up in the hospital and felt even worse that she was still alive and left her babies not knowing if they were still dead or alive. June's father gives her an envelope with a feather of a swan inside that came from Suyuan. Then her father tells June that Suyuan couldn't give the feather to her at the time because Suyuan felt like she wasn't worthy as a mother to give the swan feather to June.

Her father then opened up to June saying that Suyuan gave up hope when she left her twin babies in China. How was Suyuan able to give hope to June when Suyuan had lost it after what happened in China? When Suyuan gave birth to June, her hope was back again along with the hope of her twins' survival, which she transferred to June. You see June travel to China and meet her twin sisters for the first time. She tells her sisters the truth about Suyuan and tells them how much Suyuan loves them. June also mentions that she is taking the place of her mother in bringing her twin sisters hope. When the twin sisters learn that June is their little sister, they cry and hug each other. June realizes that she was able to fulfill her mother's wish, which is to reunite with her long-lost sisters.

Suyuan and June both felt like a disappointment to each other. Suyuan felt as a mother she wasn't worthy to June because of what happened to her twin daughters in China. June felt like a constant disappointment to Suyuan because she didn't live up to her expectations. Suyuan did love her daughter and she was finally able to tell June that she does see her for who really is. They were able to mend their relationship before Suyuan passed away and June was able to find out the truth about her twin sisters from her father.

Lindo and Waverly

As Lindo starts to think about how Suyuan just left her twin girls to come to America, she starts thinking about her own life in China. When Lindo was 4 years old, she was going to be married off at the age of 15 to Huang Tai Tai's son, a lady that Lindo's mother made the arrangement with. The reason why her mother made that arrangement was to give Lindo a better life since the Huangs were a wealthy family. Lindo became a dutiful wife in a loveless marriage. She also was harassed and abused by her mother-in-law for not producing any grandsons and calling Lindo a bad wife. Eventually, Lindo was able to con her way out of the loveless marriage and was able to move to Shanghai.

Then you fast forward to Lindo's life in America. Lindo picks up the phone and gets a call from her daughter, Waverly, saying she cannot go to the salon with her. Of course, Lindo gets angry and guilt trips Waverly into going. As Waverly sits and waits for Lindo to get her hair done at the salon, she starts saying:

> *My mom always does this. Whatever I say, whatever I do, whatever I think, she has always has the perfect countermove. As if she had been the chess champion.*

As a child, Waverly was a chess prodigy and chess made her show up as her confident self. Her mother would always show off Waverly's chess abilities to others. Lindo would walk around the neighborhood holding a copy of Waverly in a cover of the magazine showing it off to everyone. Waverly was embarrassed that Lindo would use her to show off to others, and because of it, she decided to quit playing chess. Lindo was furious and pretended that Waverly never played chess. Waverly wanted to play chess again and competed at another tournament, but because Lindo paid no attention to her, she ended up losing all her confidence and lost the tournament. From then on, Waverly never played chess again.

When Waverly became an adult, she did everything she could to please her mother. She married a Chinese man and gave her a granddaughter, but it wasn't enough for Lindo. When Waverly divorced her husband, Lindo was upset and made it seem like it was Waverly's fault that this happened.

Waverly started living with her new fiancé Rich and wanted to get approval from Lindo. She brings Rich to Lindo's birthday party, thinking he could win her over. The dinner party turned out to be a disaster because Rich did not follow the dinner rituals, used the chopsticks wrong, insulted Lindo's cooking, and drank a whole cup of wine when everyone else only had a sip.

Back at the salon, as Lindo is getting her hair done in preparation for Waverly's wedding, you can see the mother and daughter thinking they are not good enough for each other. Waverly thinks anything she does will not please her mother, and Lindo thinks her daughter is ashamed of her. Lindo starts to cry and starts talking about her last memories with her own mother. Waverly finally tells Lindo that anything she does, she feels like it's never enough for her mother. After hearing this, Lindo tells Waverly how hearing that makes her happy, and they both start to laugh.

In this story, you see a young Lindo thinking she wasn't good enough for her mother because she gave her away to be married off at such a young age. She felt abandoned by her own mother when in reality, Lindo's mother wanted a better life for her. They lived as peasants and being married off to a wealthier family meant a better life for Lindo.

As Lindo became a mother herself, she showed off to everyone that Waverly was a chess prodigy. The more she showed off Waverly, the more embarrassed Waverly got and finally told Lindo that she would never play chess again. Lindo decided to not pay attention to anything Waverly did to protect herself from getting hurt again. It was bad enough that Lindo was hurt when her mom gave her up as a teenager and even worse that her own daughter is embarrassed of her.

Waverly also felt like she wasn't good enough for Lindo. Anything Waverly did to please her mother, she felt like it was never enough. Because each generation never spoke of the true reasons, there was always a big miscommunication and the same sentiments of not being a good enough daughter for their mother was transferred to the next generation.

It wasn't until Waverly and Lindo opened up to each other that they were able to mend their relationship as mother and daughter. They were able to break the cycle.

Ying-Ying and Lena

Ying-Ying's story starts in China as a single girl who falls in love with a handsome man who later becomes her husband and has a son. Her husband turned out to be abusive and a cheater. Because she was depressed at the fact her husband took everything away from her, she accidentally killed her son while giving him a bath. The day Ying-Ying accidentally killed her son was also the day her spirit left her.

Years later, Ying-Ying moves to America, remarries, and has a daughter named Lena. Even though she has a better life in America, Ying-Ying still carries the pain of losing her son.

Because of this, Ying-Ying feels that Lena had no spirit since she had none to give her.

Lena never knew what happened to her mother, even though she knew it was a bad situation. The only thing Ying-Ying told Lena was that she was involved with a bad man in China. Ying-Ying also worries that Lena will end up like her.

Ying-Ying starts to get better and seems to resolve the trauma she went through in China. She visits Lena and her husband, Harold (who is also her boss), in their new home and notices the financial arrangement that Lena and her husband have on the fridge.

Lena starts to narrate about her financial arrangement with her husband and how everything is split 50/50 as a sign that they are equals. On the surface it may look like it's 50/50 but it's not. There is one scene where Harold and Lena had dinner and split the bill 50/50, but Lena mentions in her head that she only ate a salad and Harold's meal cost three times more than hers. She also mentions how Harold makes seven and a half times more than her and yet everything is still split 50/50.

She even got a cat from Harold as a birthday present, and he still bills her when she has to get rid of the cat's fleas. Among other things, Lena has to split the bill for ice cream even though she doesn't eat ice cream. Ying-Ying sees this and voices out her opinions as to why Lena has to pay for ice cream when she doesn't eat it.

Ying-Ying realizes that her daughter is in a marriage where she is disrespected by her husband, which was the same thing that happened to her in China. She knows that she has to fix the situation before it's too late for Lena. Ying-Ying encourages Lena to confront her husband and tell him what she wants or leave him. In the next scene, you see a happier version of Lena, one who is full of energy and spirit and beside her is a new man who respects her.

As an Asian woman, you are so good at hiding your pain. We never want to tell anyone the bad stuff that happened to us. Instead we keep it to ourselves so that we can protect it from our offspring. What we don't realize is that the pain carries on and if we don't open up, the same situation will happen to the next generation. Just like Ying-Ying and Lena, both were in a marriage where the husbands had no respect for their wives. Because Ying-Ying was in so much pain from losing her son in China and angry at her husband for taking everything away from her, she became depressed and could not give any hope to Lena. Ying-Ying was in a state of trying to come out of her own trauma.

An-Mei and Rose

An-Mei starts her story with having no recollection of her own mother. Her mother was kicked out of the house when An-Mei was 4 years old for breaking her vow as a widow. After An-Mei's father passed away, her mother became a fourth wife of Wu-Tsing, a wealthy man. An-Mei was taught by her grandparents, uncles, and aunties to hate her mother for what she did.

Years later, An-Mei reunites with her mother.

In America, An-Mei is at the grocery store with her daughter, Rose. You learn about Rose and how she meets her husband Ted who comes from a liberal white family. When Ted introduces Rose to his parents during a party they are hosting, you can see in their faces that they are less than thrilled to meet her but fake it.

Ted's mother then approaches Rose and tells her basically that because Rose is Asian, she doesn't fit in Ted's world. The mother even mentions to Rose that this is the way the world works and because Vietnam was unpopular due to the Vietnam War, Rose then interrupts her saying that she is not Vietnamese, she is American. Ted walks into their conversation and speaks up for Rose. Both Rose and Ted walk out of the party.

Six months later, Rose and Ted got married, and soon Rose realizes the pressure she had to go through being Ted's wife. Rose became the dutiful and selfless wife as a way of showing Ted her love for him even though he never asked her to do that. Rose did everything to make Ted happy and forgot to make herself happy. She was offered an art program that she wanted to participate in but in her head, she knew she couldn't go because she thought her husband needed her to attend his every need.

Their love grew apart the more she became the dutiful wife; she even had a daughter with him as a last hope that their marriage would last. In one scene, Rose walks into Ted's office asking him what he wanted to have for dinner, and Ted tells her to choose whatever she wanted. Instead of Rose choosing something that she wanted to eat, she keeps giving Ted different choices for dinner. Ted gets fed up and tells Rose that for once, he just wants to know what she wants for herself. He misses the Rose that spoke up and was opinionated.

Rose later finds out that Ted is having an affair with another woman and decides to get a divorce. The movie takes us to An-Mei and Rose talking. Rose has made Ted's favorite peanut butter pie and An-Mei asks her what she will do with the leftovers if he only eats one slice. An-Mei wants Rose to see her worth, but Rose doesn't see it. Then An-Mei tells Rose that she is like her grandmother who never saw her worth as a woman and a wife.

The movie goes back to An-Mei as a child and moves in with her mother. An-Mei was so happy to be with her mom and her new home until she met her stepfather, his children, and his many wives. An-Mei's mother was the fourth wife in the household. As An-Mei saw all the wives walk into the house, she noticed that the second wife was the only one who had a son. She also noticed that something was off because she saw how her mother was looking at the boy.

An-Mei found out from the nanny that the second wife lured her mother to the house to play mahjong. Instead of playing mahjong, she was raped by Wu-Tsing. Nobody believed An-Mei's mother was raped, and she was disowned by her own family thinking she was a concubine. Historically, Asian women constantly take the blame for something they're not responsible for. With no choice left and being pregnant, An-Mei went back to Wu-Tsing's house and second wife took her in but it came with a high price. When An-Mei's mother gave birth to a baby boy, the second wife took the baby and claimed it as her own.

An-Mei found her mother dead, and the second wife told her it was from a drug overdose. She knew that her mother killed herself on purpose and told An-Mei before she died that she killed her own spirit so she could give An-Mei a stronger one. During the funeral ceremony, An-Mei took her brother and threatened Wu-Tsing to pay for his sins or something horrible would happen to him. On that day, Wu-Tsing honored An-Mei's mother as his first and only wife. He also promised to raise An-Mei and her brother as his honored children, which is the highest position. An-Mei had the strength to speak up for the injustice that happened to her mother.

Rose starts to ask An-Mei what all this means. An-Mei tells her:

> *I tell you the story because I was raised the Chinese way. I was taught to desire nothing, to swallow other people's misery and to eat my own bitterness. And even though I taught my daughter the opposite, but still she came out the same way. Maybe it is because she was born to me and she was born a girl. And I was born to my mother, and I was born a girl. All of us like stairs, one step after another, going up, going down, but always going the same way.*

An-Mei wants Rose to see her worth before it's too late. An-Mei doesn't want Rose to go through the same path as her mother. It was the first time Rose was able to see her worth and she kicks her husband out of the house for what he did. Rose finally tells

Ted that he is not taking anything from her anymore and starts to tell him that her grandmother died 60 years ago from an opium overdose in order to save her daughter. She finally tells Ted that it wasn't his fault that she felt like her love for him wasn't good enough. She opened up to Ted saying she felt that his love was worth more than hers and realized it was all in her head. She took herself for granted because she didn't see her own worth. In the next scene, you see Rose and Ted get back together.

In this story, you see how An-Mei's mother felt worthless because of what happened to her and that she had to kill herself to give strength to her daughter. While An-Mei was stronger and was able to speak up for her and her brother, her daughter Rose went through the same path as her grandmother. As soon as An-Mei realized what was happening to her own daughter, she knew she had to save her daughter from going down the same path. You can see that Rose was carrying the trauma of her grandmother and felt unworthy as well. Rose also felt she wasn't good enough as a wife when it was far from the truth.

You also see how in Chinese society, An-Mei's mother was labeled as a whore even though she was raped by Wu-Tsing. She was disowned from her own family and seen as trash because of it. This also led to her feeling small and not knowing her worth because everyone around her told her she was worthless, just like when Ted's mother went up to Rose and told her she wouldn't be a good fit for Ted because she was Asian.

I actually watched *The Joy Luck Club* again just for the sole purpose of writing this chapter because I really wanted to dissect each of their stories to provide the best information for you.

What I didn't realize was that I was going to be crying so much after watching the movie, but it's definitely a movie to watch because it does showcase the complex relationships Asian mothers and daughters have and the intergenerational trauma that comes with it.

I hope by reading this chapter you're able to talk to your parents and have an open conversation about the traumas they went through and see if there is a pattern that is stopping you from moving forward in your life. It may be hard for them to open up because of your upbringing, but it will help you and your family understand each other a lot better. Like these women and their daughters were able to have a better relationship because they were able to open up and have an honest conversation.

While intergenerational trauma is a topic that must be addressed, it is not the only form of trauma that you may have gone through, and in the next chapter, I will start to share about other kinds of trauma that can happen and how to unlock the feelings to move forward in your life.

4

How to Unlock Our Traumas

When I was about 11 or 12 years old, I was walking to the library when an older Caucasian man bumped into me. He was probably in his 40s, and all I could remember was that he had a mustache.

At the time, I thought it was my fault that I bumped into him but something felt off. When the man bumped into me, he was in my personal space for a good amount of time to touch me and my body. When he was done, he walked away, but he turned his head back and looked at me with this evil smile, like he was so satisfied to feel me up. I'm not too sure how to describe it, but that man's smile has haunted me till this day.

I never told anybody because I felt so ashamed that something like that happened to me, like it was my fault. How was I supposed to know at that age what that man did was inappropriate? For the longest time, I forgot that this incident happened to me. I locked it away like it never happened. It was actually the height of the #MeToo movement that triggered me to remember this incident happened. When I started seeing women sharing their stories of how they were sexually assaulted or harassed, my own incident started to pop back into my head, and instead of feeling shame, I realized I wasn't the only woman who had gone through something like this.

Everyone has a story to tell and sharing these situations is never easy. There are all kinds of feelings that come up. You feel uncomfortable, embarrassed, and ashamed. Sometimes you feel like the world will judge you for hiding something for so long, especially when you are empowering your Asian sisters to speak up. There is also a feeling of relief that something you have been keeping for so long is out of the bag. At least, that's what I feel now sharing this with you.

It's quite scary to share something that I have never told anyone in my life. This has been a secret that I have kept for over 25 years because of the shame that I felt. Not even my closest friends or my family knew this happened to me. This is the first time I'm sharing this to the world, and it's quite scary to share such a deep secret that you have kept for so long. I thought being strong was to not share what I went through and just keep it in because it was taught in my culture for so long.

I know now that in order to be a leader, I also have to lead by example. Not being able to share this story is selfish on my part because there is someone out there reading this book who can heal in her own journey. If I can share my story, then someone else will have the courage to share her story, and it becomes a domino effect. I want you to never feel ashamed of something you weren't responsible for.

You may have traumas you never knew existed or worse, you are carrying the burden of someone else's trauma. Your traumas can stop you from moving forward and becoming the person you are meant to be. It's also uncomfortable when you have to go through something like this, but it's important to get comfortable with the uncomfortable so that you can move forward and become your better self. Let's begin this chapter about traumas.

What Is Trauma?

I think the first and most important thing you have to tackle is the definition of trauma. Some of you may not realize that what you are experiencing is some form of trauma. According to *Very Well Mind*, the definition of trauma is any emotional, physical, or psychological event or experience that causes distress for a person and can also affect a person's ability to cope and function properly.[1]

Every single person has faced some form of trauma. This is something that is not typical in Asian culture. It's difficult to talk about the traumas you go through because you were told to keep it to yourself. That doesn't help yourself or anyone else. This is why you suffer so much and think you are not good enough to be anything else.

Not being able to deal with traumas is the core reason why people deal with so many mental health issues.

Here's some data shared from *InnerBody Research*, one of the largest home health and wellness guides online, reaching more than 2 million readers a month, about women's mental health status:

- Depression is one of the most widespread mental illnesses, affecting up to 5% of adults worldwide.
- Women experience depression twice as much as men.
- The COVID-19 pandemic created a 25% increase in anxiety disorders worldwide, and the most affected were children and women.
- Posttraumatic stress disorder (PTSD) affects 10% of women, and 4% of men.
- Calls from people seeking help with eating disorders increased 70% since 2020.
- Eating disorders increase a woman's mortality rate, which leads to higher medical costs and shorter life spans.

- Alcohol abuse accounts for a 50% to 100% higher death rates among women than men.
- Thirteen percent of Americans started or increased their use of drugs since June 2020.
- Suicide is the 12th leading cause of death in the United States.
- Two-thirds of people diagnosed with dementia are women.[2]

Childhood Trauma

You don't realize that you can experience trauma from the moment you are born. Most people think that babies and toddlers aren't aware of their surroundings, but you would be surprised how much a baby or infant's brain can intake information from past traumatic experiences.[3]

Your brain is your hard drive. Whatever you see as a child goes into your subconscious. When you fill your computer hard drive with good stuff, your computer will work well. When you fill your computer hard drive with bad stuff, the computer will know it's a virus, and it won't work properly. It's important to know that from the time a child is born, the child will be aware of the things they say, the things they see, and the things they experience.

A child can go through many different traumas in their lifetime. Some of the traumas that a child may have experienced are being bullied by their peers or elders; sexually, mentally, and physically abused; trafficked into the sex industry; forced to do something they are not comfortable with; medical trauma such as being sick, racists attacks, or loss of a loved one; parents going through a divorce; being neglected or abandoned, and alcohol or substance abuse.

Some children witness incidents of violence against Asians and Asian Americans in the United States. One incident that stuck out for me was the 5-year-old girl who saw her father get punched in an unprovoked racially motivated attack.[4]

If this girl doesn't get professional help in processing this traumatic event, she might develop mental health issues as she grows older.

Another article I read was about a Filipino restaurant owner in Oakland who was shot and killed in front of his 11-year-old son.[5] If the son also doesn't get the help he needs, he might go through life hating everybody because of what happened to his father. Time and again, studies and history show that children or young adults who witness violence often get involved in violent incidents themselves when they become adults.[6]

These two scenarios may be heavier than most, but it doesn't mean you don't take the small traumas lightly. I think it's important to always talk to your kids about the situations that happen to them and have a safe and open space where they can let out how they feel.

I know if I had an outlet to talk about the traumas that I was going through as a child, I would have been more willing to go out and be more confident in myself and my abilities. As I mentioned, for years I thought I was a total failure because I failed kindergarten when I was five years old for coloring outside the lines. I had no time to process what happened to me as a child. I was transferred to a different school and started kindergarten all over again. For most of my life, I thought I was a constant failure and resisted taking action in my life because of that fear of failure.

It wasn't until I attended a self-development event in Hawaii where I was able to unlock my trauma that was hidden for so long. By doing certain exercises during this event, I was able to dig deep and realize why I thought I was a constant failure in my own life. (Hint: it was because I failed kindergarten.)

If I did the work and spoke about this to someone, I could have realized that I was never meant to color inside the lines. I was always meant to do something outside of the box instead of following what my culture told me to do.

This was a huge wake-up moment for me. I felt so much lighter after that huge realization, which was 30 years after it happened. From that moment, I saw failure as a way of producing a result. If attempt 32 did not work, then I move onto 33 or until I get it right.

PTSD

When you hear the term PTSD, or posttraumatic stress disorder, you think this is something that only soldiers deal with after they have been discharged from the military. PTSD does not happen only to soldiers; it can also happen to anyone, and sometimes you don't realize you've experienced PTSD.

PTSD is also called shell shock or battle fatigue syndrome. It's a serious condition that can develop "*after a person has experienced or witnessed a traumatic or terrifying event in which there was serious physical harm or threat*."[7]

Every person deals with PTSD in different ways. An article from WebMD mentioned the common signs of PTSD:

- Experiencing flashbacks of the traumatic experience by having nightmares or re-enacting the past event
- Avoiding talking about what happened in the past
- Having erratic behavior such as having a more intense emotion or have outburst out of nowhere
- Experiencing unexpected mood swings that can be unrelated to the traumatic event.[8]

Other symptoms can include not sleeping well, things or people who may trigger you, mental health issues, and even thoughts of suicide.

What's even worse is that some people will not go through PTSD until years later when a person or event may trigger it. If you don't have the tools and resources to talk about your PTSD, it can literally disrupt everything in your life. Here's the latest statistics on PTSD from the Center for Advancing Health:

- Three in every 50 Americans will go or have gone through PTSD in their lifetime.
- The leading cause of PTSD is sexual violence.
- Of women who were sexually abused, 94% develop PTSD symptoms during the first two weeks after the trauma.
- Thirty percent of women still experience PTSD symptoms 9 months after the trauma.
- Women suffer from PTSD more than men.
- About 12 million American adults suffer from PTSD in any year.
- The 45–59 age group suffers from PTSD the most.
- Eleven out of 20 military women experience sexual harassment during their time in the military.[9]

People who have suffered from PTSD has committed suicide, been labeled as mentally ill, has been cast out from friends and family, and have turned to alcohol and substance abuse.[10]

The Asian community has been faced with PTSD for centuries, especially Asian women, whether it's a racist attack, being sexually assaulted, or being seen as less than a human being. This sets you back from moving forward in your life.

There are four most common causes of PTSD: sexual violence, war and conflict, natural disasters, and intimate partner violence.[11]

Sexual Violence

This is the most common cause of PTSD. Sexual violence can come in many forms, such as rape, sex trafficking, incest, child sexual violence, sexual violence from a partner, and stalking. Sexual violence is any sexual contact that is forced or not wanted by the victim. This usually happens to women and children, and most violent sexual crimes are not reported because of the shame or humiliation that the victim feels. Usually the victim feels like it's their fault that the incident happened.

War and Conflict

When you hear the term PTSD, you normally associate this with veterans and what they have gone through serving in a war. You have seen movies where veterans go through erratic behavior or get flashbacks of their days during battle. Sometimes you see them start to think they are re-enacting the battle they experienced during their military service. The Recovery Village shared that 71% of female military members experience PTSD because of sexual assault within the ranks.[12]

Natural Disasters

If you have never gone through a natural disaster, you don't know how it feels to have everything gone in a blink of an eye. You lose the ones you love, and you have to start back at square one.

In December 2021, Typhoon Odette hit the Philippines and destroyed the city where I was born. I couldn't contact my friends and family for days because there was no electricity or power. I was starting to get worried, especially about my grandmothers since they were a lot older. I had friends tell me they had to wake up at 3 a.m. everyday just to go out and drive to find gas since there was a shortage. I had friends who lost their homes, had to hide in closets during the typhoon, and emerged to find their stores shattered, and they were considered the lucky ones. There were poor people who had nothing to begin with and were left with nothing after the typhoon. They had no way to get themselves back to rebuilding their lives and it felt like all hope was gone. In all of my years living in my city of Cebu, I had never seen a disaster like that in my life ever.

Intimate Partner Violence

This is very common in the Asian community. Asian women are being abused since they are treated like property instead of of human beings. In many Asian cultures, the religious practices, the political regime, and the history of traditions for Asian women are some of the main factors of why intimate partner violence is prevalent. Asian mail order brides and child marriages are more prevalent that you think, and this is a form of human trafficking.[13] Once a person sees you as property, they do as they please because of it. There is definitely lasting negative effects when you experience intimate partner abuse. Many women will end up committing suicide, or they may start an alcohol or drug addiction because of the pent-up anger and frustration they have faced in the past.[14]

Intimate partner violence was more prevalent during the pandemic. UN Women coined this as the Shadow Pandemic during COVID-19 and reported that one in three women experience sexual and physical abuse by an intimate partner.[15]

The rise of anti-Asian hate from the pandemic has been a major cause of PTSD, especially for Asian women. The fact that you cannot be safe in your own city makes you constantly paranoid that somebody is ready to jump you. Fear has been the trigger for Asian women and the elderly. It doesn't help that Asian women are seen as quiet, submissive, and obedient, which makes them an easy target for anti-Asian hate crimes.

I have spoken with Asian women who live in New York and California, and they have personally told me that they are constantly looking over their shoulder to make sure that nobody is following them or to avoid a surprise attack.

Let's not forget the subliminal violence toward Asians during the pandemic. A prime example is when the news media uses an accompanying photo of Asian women in a mask (they particularly like using images of women) every time they publish updates on COVID-19 variants, and the photo is right on the front page in the center of the article so that everyone can see it.

Not only do you live in constant fear for yourself, you also live in fear for your loved ones as well. Every time I hear that an elderly person was attacked, I fear that it could be my mother, grandmother, or auntie. When my parents call me and tell me they are going out to get groceries or even out for a walk, I already start getting scared and paranoid thinking of the worst that can happen even though they live in a safe neighborhood. I fear for one of my good friend's mom who likes to take walks by herself because an elderly Asian woman alone is the easiest target for anyone to attack at this point. This constant fear and paranoia can get to you especially since it's all you ever see and hear about in the media.

A report from the American Psychiatric Association mentioned that 70% of Southeast Asian refugees who seek mental health treatment were diagnosed with PTSD.[16]

PTSD can negatively affect you. It can stop you from speaking up and moving forward to forge your own path. For women, especially, life-changing decisions could be affected by mental health issues such as PTSD. If you don't have the proper tools and resources to help, you will end up living in constant fear.

Racial Trauma

Since the beginning of the COVID-19 pandemic, the Asian community has been the blame for it. The rise of terms such as "China virus" or "kung flu" coined by former President Donald Trump, no less, fueled xenophobia and enabled the rise of anti-Asian violence and crimes.

However, it's important to acknowledge that anti-Asian hate and violence is deeply rooted in history. Ever since our Asian ancestors landed in the United States and Canada, the community went through the Chinese Exclusion Act, Japanese internment camps, and more. Most people think that the anti-Asian racism only happened during the pandemic and that is because this information was never taught in schools.

I talked at a company for Asian Heritage Month and showed a timeline of how Asian Canadians were treated in Canada. Most people were shocked with the information that was shared, such as Chinese people had to pay a head tax just to enter the country that would amount to the price of two homes. Imagine if you had to do that today; the average price of a house in Toronto is $1 million. That is a huge amount to pay just to get into the country.

A report from Stop AAPI Hate shared the latest report of anti-Asian hate crimes and how it has affected our communities:

- Forty-nine percent of the AAPI community feel safe going out.
- Sixty-five percent of the AAPI community worry about the safety of their family members, especially the elderly.
- Thirty-two percent of AAPI parents worry about their children becoming a target of anti-Asian racist attacks in unsupervised places.
- Ninety-five percent of the AAPI community who reported a hate crime view the United States as more dangerous for them.
- Ninety-eight percent of AAPI elders who experienced a racist attack feel like the United States is physically dangerous for our community.
- Forty-nine percent of the AAPI community report depression and anxiety.
- Seventy-two percent of the AAPI community report discrimination as a cause of stress.[17]

In Canada, most people think that anti-Asian racism does not exist. Just in Vancouver alone, Asian women are getting attacked in broad daylight due to a hate crime, and if this isn't enough proof, the Government of Canada shared the following:

- In Vancouver, there was an 878% increase in reported hate crimes since 2019.
- The Ottawa police experienced a 600% increase of reported anti-Asian hate crimes, while the Montreal police reported five times more and the Toronto police reported 51% more.
- Canada continues to report a higher per capita rate of anti-Asian hate crimes than the United States by more than 100%.[18]

These numbers are based on crimes that are reported. Imagine how many crimes are unreported in Canada and the United States. The Asian community also contributes to the problem because the culture has been ingrained to never talk about the bad situations that happened to you. You are told to keep it to yourself, thinking it won't happen again, but this silence is also the main reason why the Asian community is constantly being targeted.

I had an aunt who was walking along downtown Toronto, and she was spat on by a random person walking. She never mentioned it to anyone until months later.

With the huge increase of racial hate crimes, the worst part about all of this is that nobody seems to care about what is happening to the Asian community. An opinion article from the *Daily Bruin* is a great reason why there is poor coverage when it comes to anti-Asian hate crimes. Some of the biggest reasons dates back centuries. Asian Americans have been seen as a threat to the US empire, and it's one of the main reasons why there were laws such as the Chinese Exclusion Act, Japanese internment camps, and even denying US citizenship to Asian immigrants.

The model minority myth is another reason for the poor coverage of hate crimes against the Asian community. Also, when most people talk about underrepresented communities, Asian Americans are not on the list. Most of the time, countries like the United States and Canada don't see Asians as "oppressed" because Asians are seen as successful and don't require any help.[19]

I have a group chat with some fellow Asian colleagues who are passionate about diversion, equity, and inclusion (DEI) efforts for the Asian community, but when you see companies promote DEI panel sessions, we all noticed that Asians are left out of this equation. You see African Americans, Caucasians, and Latinos represented in the DEI panel but not one Asian person. Most companies fail to see that Asian Americans are one of the underrepresented communities. Asian Americans aren't even seen as "people of color" because of our pale skin and the model minority myth. Even this article from Reuters talks about Amazon creating its first venture fund for underrepresented groups, except Asians:

> *The online retailer said it is aiming to put money into more than 10 funds supporting some 200 companies at or before the seed stage of investment, through 2023. It is focused on Black, Latino, female, Indigenous and lesbian, gay, bisexual, transgender, queer, intersex and asexual (LGBTQIA+) founders.*[20]

During the Atlanta shooting in March 2021, NBC News had a press panel to discuss the anti-Asian violence and the panel was made up of two white men, two white women, and one black man. When I saw this panel, I was totally disappointed. More than 24 million Asian Americans and they couldn't put one Asian person in the panel. This is how invisible the Asian community feels most of the time.

In general, there's very little empathy for and understanding of just how much racial micro-aggressions, such as insensitive remarks or off-hand jokes, affect quality of life for people of color.

For the Asian community, the "invisibility" and the cultural tendency to stay silent make the struggle and effects even more difficult to acknowledge.

An incident that resonated with me was an article about an Asian girl who attended a Halsey concert in Irvine, California, and became a victim of hate speech from a concert goer. She was even more disappointed when nobody stepped in to help her. From that moment, she cannot listen to Halsey songs anymore because it's just a reminder of what happened to her.[21]

When I was a kid, one of the things I wanted to do was to go to IHOP. I would see commercials on TV and beg my parents to go there the next time we drive to America.

We usually drive to Buffalo back in the day because it was only a two-hour drive from Toronto. My parents took us to eat at IHOP on one of our road trips, and I was on cloud nine. I was so excited to finally get those pancakes that I saw in the commercials.

When we were seated at our table, it was downhill from there. First off, we were the only Asian family in the restaurant. There was one black family, and the rest of the people were white. Our waitress was far from nice. She hardly looked at us, and she served the other tables before us even though we arrived there first.

The whole experience was terrible. The waitress didn't treat us as customers at all. When we were about to leave the restaurant, the hostess asked my mother how the service was. My mom answered:

> *The service was bad, I think it was because of the color of our skin.*

The hostess was in total shock that my Asian mother had the balls to say that to her. She couldn't even respond back. I think she had no idea what to say after that comment. We left the restaurant and from that moment, I told myself I would never set foot in an IHOP ever again. Every time I would see an IHOP sign, all I ever feel is anger and frustration, even now, because of how racist the waitress was to us.

Asian women are the most affected from the anti-Asian hate crimes. There has been a huge rise of violence against Asian women, and it's putting us on the edge. Asian women have become more paranoid and fearful of our surroundings because of it. When I traveled to the United States in May 2022, I was starting to get scared for my own well-being.

I had all these disturbing thoughts in my head thinking of the worst things that could happen to me. I almost didn't want to walk by myself because I was afraid that I was going to be an easy target, especially traveling to Oakland, California, since there were frequent reports of Asian women and elderly being attacked there. I think it's normal to feel this way when all you see in the media is attack after attack, and it can truly affect how we think or feel.

Money Trauma

For Asian women, money plays a huge factor in their trauma, especially when growing up. When you grow up in a culture where you are seen as second best to men, you are sometimes left with nothing, and that can take a toll on your mental well-being.

Women have shared stories with me that because the men control the finances in the relationship, the women feel shameful to even ask for $5 dollars just to go buy something. I remember my grandmother from my mom's side telling me how when she was married to my grandfather, she would save up every single dollar that she was given just to buy her own things. This has made her afraid to ask for money from anyone, even if it's her own money. She feels ashamed that she has to ask when it shouldn't be shameful to begin with.

Financial abuse is prevalent in Asian countries, especially when you grow up in a poor household. How many times are you forced to do something you don't want to do just so you can provide food on the table for your loved ones? In the Philippines, this is more normal than you realize.

Young women and children are forced into prostitution so they can feed their families. Women are abused by their partners and are told never to say a word, or they will be left with nothing. This is a sad reality that Asian women face and is rarely talked about. If we don't educate the women about how to be financially independent, the cycle will continue to future generations.

I was fortunate enough to have parents who helped me learn to become financially independent. They taught me how to save and how to invest my money. Saving money was ingrained in my head as a child. Every dollar I received, I would put it in my piggy bank until it was time for me to open my first bank account.

I remember as a teenager when I asked my mom to buy me something, she told me, "If you want to buy something for yourself, it's time for you to get a job."

And I did just that. My first job was working as a sales associate at Walmart. Working part-time made me value money more and realize that it's not always easy to make, especially when you earned minimum wage in 1998 which was $6.85 an hour at the time.

As I grew older, I thought working hard at an office job would bring me success because that is all I ever knew. I did that for 12 years thinking that was the best I could do as an Asian woman. I put in long hours, never took vacation, and worked to the bone just to get, if I was lucky, a 3% raise each year due to the inflation rate. Is this what success is supposed to look like for me?

When my aunt passed away from a horrific accident, I realized how short life is and that your life can be taken away at any moment. So from then on, I wanted to forge my own path so that I could live with no regrets. This is what led me to entrepreneurship.

Going into entrepreneurship wasn't easy for me. As an Asian woman, I was too afraid to ask people for money because the Asian culture constantly tells you that asking for money was considered shameful. I remember babysitting for my aunt, and she gave me a $50 gas card as payment, and my dad asked me why I took it, like I did something wrong. So when I would talk to potential clients, I was either too afraid to ask for money or just gave an amount so low that I literally gave away my offer.

This is common for Asian women and most women in general. You tend to lower the price of your products and services, or you just give everything away because you feel like you're not good enough. The more you don't value yourself, the more other people will not value you.

It wasn't until I started to build my confidence and I raised my prices and people valued me for the work I did. If anyone tried to discount my work, I turned them away because it wasn't worth my time.

Sometimes you have money traumas that come from your parents and grandparents. I always wondered why my grandmother from my dad's side was always very cautious with her spending. I never understood why it was so hard for her to spend her money. It wasn't until my aunt told me that when she was married to my grandfather, he had a spending problem to the point where banks were calling my grandmother to collect money.

My grandmother is the type of person who never wants to share her problems with anyone, not even her family, but when you live in a city where everybody knows everybody, people knew what was happening. My great grandfather found out about my grandmother's money problems and was able to bail her out. I think till this day, my grandmother is still traumatized by this incident.

If you and your family migrate to the United States or Canada, you often come with nothing and have to start from the bottom.

You have to penny pinch for every single expense just to survive and live the American Dream. I've heard so many stories of Asian immigrants who migrate to the West with nothing more than $30 in their pocket and a dream. Because most Asian parents lived like this, they tell you to never live beyond your means.

They fear that if you spend all your money, then you will be left with nothing. They fear the uncertainty of not having enough money when that can be far from the truth. When you grow up in an Asian household, I have noticed that most people end up being two extremes when it comes to spending money. You either save every penny like your parents or want to spend every penny because you were deprived of the things you wanted as a child.

Neither are great in my opinion. The one extreme where you save every single penny and end up doing nothing because you are too afraid to spend money—what quality of life are you living? This is not the way to live your life especially when you are here for such a short period.

At the other extreme, you spend every single dollar you make buying unnecessary items, and you end up broke or in debt because you just wanted to buy the things you never got as a child. This is also not a way to live because it becomes an addiction that stems from your childhood.

This is just what I have observed. I am not a financial expert, and I don't claim to be. I have a financial advisor who gives me advice on what to do with my money. I have also become someone who practices a good balance of spending. I know when I want to spend and when to stop.

The pandemic has also affected money trauma. When the whole world locks down and you cannot go to work because of it, you start to stress out and constantly worry about how you are going to pay for the bills or even put a roof over your head.

This situation affected women way more than men because some women had to make the hard decision to quit their jobs to home school their children. Some women had to take lower paying jobs just to make ends meet. Women were often the ones who ran the household, took care of the kids at home 24/7, and still worked a full-time job and/or business. In one year, CNBC reported that women globally lost a total income of $800 billion from the pandemic, which is the combined GDP of 98 countries.[22]

How you view money can also be a factor of your trauma. How many times have you heard, *money is the root of all evil*?

Of course, this is not what the real Bible verse says, which makes people think that money is evil and anything to do with money, people want nothing to do with it because of this one statement. Money isn't evil. Money can help build schools for the less fortunate, save people from natural disasters. You can use money for good if you choose to. Of course there are bad people out there who use money for their personal gain and this is where the Bible verse from Timothy 6:10 is misunderstood:

> *For the love of money is the root of all evil: which while some coveted after, they have erred from the faith, and pierced themselves through with many sorrows.*

Greed and corruption are evil. Utilizing money to fuel that greed and corruption is when it becomes evil, not money itself. Many people think money is evil, which is misleading and creates a totally misconstrued perception of money that doesn't serve you.

Money can also be empowering, especially when a woman is financially independent. While it is great for women to be financially independent, it can also be seen as unattractive to men. A woman will decide to quit her high-paying job, stop going to an Ivy League school, or stop running her business to get married and run the household because that has more importance in Asian culture.

Money trauma can play a huge factor in your life, particularly how you spend money, how you view money, and your relationship with money. Most of this stems from your culture, which I will explain more next.

Cultural Trauma

As an Asian woman, you have to live by so many rules within your culture. You are told what to do, what to say, how to dress, how you are supposed to live your life, and if you do anything outside of that, you are seen as weird or out of character.

This becomes exhausting as well since you always have to make an appearance and never talk about the issues you go through. The need to be perfect, the need to always follow traditions that don't make sense, and the standards you have to live by can take a huge toll on you.

How many times have you been told to never say anything bad that happens to you because you have to save face or never tarnish the family name? You cannot show up as your true self because of it. Any bad experiences you go through you keep to yourself because you end up being the bad guy, and you always have to appear as if you have no emotions and everything is perfectly fine.

I know one rule that you have been told by your Asian elders is to respect the hierarchy. Now I have no problem respecting my elders if it makes sense. Your elders aren't always right, and it can be frustrating that just because they are older than you, you have to follow what they say.

And if you don't follow what your elders say, you get the Asian elder guilt trip where they make you feel so bad that you end up doing what they tell you to do. You know the feeling: like you are being unreasonable for saying no, and they make you feel like you're the worst person in the world for standing your ground.

They say the right words to make you feel like crap, and you just end up letting them win because of the mind tricks they play.

Or you have to honor everything your parents tell you because they gave you life, and in return, you just follow what they tell you to do. If you don't follow what they say, the guilt trip also comes up.

How many times have you been in this situation? How many times have you been told that because you are the better person you should just let it go and do as you are told, not realizing that will have lasting effects on you. I've been there and done that way too many times in my life, and I felt worse every time I gave in.

What about being humble? You are told plenty of times to not brag about your accomplishments because it's tacky. When you are in business for yourself, you are shamed for promoting your products and services because it's not ladylike and you look like a beggar. How are you supposed to create an income for yourself if you don't go out and promote yourself? These are just some of the experiences you go through as an Asian woman.

Let's not forget the outdated Asian traditions you may follow and never talk about.

Nobody ever questions the traditions you honor, and you would be surprised what happens when you question your relatives as to why you do certain things in your culture; the answer is usually "Because it's tradition."

When you think about this, that is not a valid reason. There has to be an underlying reason why you do what you do. Some of these traditions were created to degrade women, and you have to call out those traditions that negatively affect Asian women or else you will keep on doing the same thing generation after generation and never break the cycle.

I know every time I would ask my aunties why we have to act on certain traditions, that's the same answer I got, and when I tried to dig deeper, they would get annoyed and just tell me to do it without any valid reason. Of course, as a good Asian woman, you just do what you are told, but for me, it didn't sit well because it didn't make sense.

Now I am not saying that all traditions are bogus. Of course there are traditions that I do follow because I understand why, but when you see something that doesn't sound right, then you have to question it.

Since the beginning of time in many cultures, a woman is seen as a burden. In China, it was commonly seen as a disappointment for families when a female baby was born because instantly it was considered an economic burden. The Confucian texts had everything to do with oppressing women. Because of Confucian rules, women went through the most ridiculous things, such as foot binding, being killed as babies, becoming one of multiples wives, becoming concubines, and widow suicide. Everything in the scriptures was written to favor men as the desired gender.[23]

And China isn't the only country in Asia that has been through ridiculous traditions. In the previous chapter I have mentioned how India treats women and created traditions that also favor men over women.

In Vietnam, Confucianism was also adopted when women were regarded as second class to men. A Vietnamese woman had to color her teeth black back in the day to show that she was married. If she was 18 years old and still not married, she was considered an old maid. Vietnamese women also had to always obey the male figure, whether it was their father, husband, or the oldest male in the household.[24]

I remember when I found the Asian mail order bride article, and it mentioned that Vietnamese women love male leadership; it made me sick to my stomach that content like that still existed in 2022. The fact is that Asian cultures shaped women to be seen as not worthy and only being good enough for the household will affect you from moving forward into being the leader you are today.

How can you move forward if you are constantly told to do everything else for others, to save face, to obey what you are told to do, and to never rock the boat? This leads to more stress, anxiety, depression, and more. It's no wonder why you suffer so much, but being able to be aware of this means you also have to learn how to unlock your traumas to move forward.

How to Unlock Your Traumas

There are many ways that trauma can show up for you. Each person is different. Here are some of the ways that I have been able to unlock my own trauma, and I hope this can help you as well.

Sometimes it could be a physical condition that you are going through. I remember when I was in my 20s, I had major canker sores everywhere in my mouth that were so painful. I had no idea why I got them, and I was worried because there were so many at the time.

I made an appointment with the dentist at the time to figure out why this was happening. The only thing he told me was that this was a sign of stress and is common. I didn't even know what I was stressing about at the time, but it was interesting that he mentioned I was getting canker sores due to stress. That stress could have come from my job, my family and friends, or from my past traumas. At the time, I didn't go through the work I have since done because it was never talked about then. Eventually the canker sores went away, and I felt at peace after.

Another way to unlock trauma is understand the triggers in your life. Sometimes you see someone or something, and you immediately get mad about it. Even something as simple as someone's name can be a trigger because maybe you knew someone else with the same name from the past who treated you badly.

It's normal to have things that trigger you, especially if you have never dealt with the traumas you are experiencing. Remember when I mentioned every time I saw the IHOP sign, I would get so mad? It was because of the racism that my family dealt with that I swore to never set foot in an IHOP ever again.

What are some of the triggers you have noticed in your life?

You also have to be aware of your current feelings. I know it's not easy to process the feelings you go through because the Asian culture constantly tells you to keep it within yourself, but that never helps you become better. With so many repressed feelings you end up becoming a ticking time bomb waiting to explode. I know because that was what happened to me during the pandemic.

When the lockdowns happened in 2020 due to the pandemic, I literally thought it was the end of the world. I had no drive to do anything, and in fact I just decided to watch K-dramas all day and eat junk food. Nobody knew what I was feeling, and I am generally a pretty private person, so sharing how I was feeling to other people was foreign to me as well. If it wasn't for my family asking me what I was going through, I wouldn't be here today sharing this with you.

I had so much pent-up feelings of paranoia, depression, and anxiety during the pandemic that I kept it to myself, thinking I had to be strong for everyone else. Sometimes it's difficult when you have a podcast talking about self-confidence and the least confident person is yourself. I thought I had to put up a front even though I was not myself at the time. This is always the case when you are told to be strong when being strong can be the hardest thing you have to be at the time.

Sometimes your greatest strength can come from being vulnerable. That was the hardest lesson for me. Being vulnerable isn't easy, and it takes courage to tell someone that you are not okay. After I was able to say that, there was so much weight lifted off from me.

Another way to unlock your trauma is learning to ask the right questions. Being able to ask yourself important questions can lead you to the right answers. When you are feeling down, the Asian Mental Health Collective recommends asking yourself these seven questions:

1. What happened in my environment that affected my mood?
2. What does this mood mean to me?
3. What can I do from now on?
4. What meaning can I introduce into my life?
5. Is this self-pity or victimization?
6. What should I try that I haven't tried?
7. If I saw someone feeling the way I am feeling right now, what would I tell that person?[25]

In the beginning of this chapter, I also mentioned the sexual harassment that I endured as a child and never mentioned to anybody because of the shame I felt even though it wasn't my fault to begin with. Most of the time you ignore your traumas, and if you ignore them, you cannot move forward because it holds you back. Being able to recount the traumas you face is important so you can find a solution to healing your traumas, which I will share in the next chapter.

5

The Journey to Healing

THE JOURNEY OF healing from your traumas will not be rainbows and unicorns. In fact, the healing process will be ugly at times, but when you can heal, you become whole again, and life becomes beautiful.

You have to remember that you are different and that your healing process will not be the same as everyone else and that is okay because you are not everyone else. Being able to know different ways to heal from your traumas can show that there isn't one way of doing things, but there are many ways to heal from your traumas. I will share with you some of the ways that I have healed from my traumas and ways other people have healed from theirs.

I think one of the biggest things I had to heal from was the need to be liked or the need to please every single person. In Asian culture, it's all you have been taught to live by, and when you constantly fear that people will not like you, it can take a toll on your mental health. This was probably the biggest trauma I had to heal from and am still healing from because when you have been taught to do this all your life, it will not go away overnight. You have to unlearn so many things in order to move forward.

Being able to heal from your traumas will help you build more confidence in yourself, be able to live in the present instead of the past, and you can start taking control of your own life. In fact, the Hawaii Youth Correctional Facility was able to report that they had no incarcerated girls in their facility because they were able to provide girls who were going through trauma in their homes due to different circumstances with healing instead of handcuffing them.[1] Hearing this makes me realize anything is possible.

Here's some things that helped me along the way that you may consider doing yourself to heal from your traumas.

Open Your Chakras

One of my biggest lessons I learned in healing was dealing with my chakras. I know you may think this may sound a little "woo-woo," and I was like you, thinking it was all ridiculous, but a good friend taught me the importance of your chakras and how you can uncover them. If you have never heard of chakras before, don't worry because I will share a crash course about it.

The first thing you need to know is what chakras are? According to the Hindu American Foundation:

> *Meaning "wheel" in Sanskrit, the term chakra (pronounced as chuh-kruh) generally refers to seven major discs of subtle energy that run along the center of the body. According to yogic texts, each chakra is related to a part of the body, and affects certain aspects of a person's life—be it creativity, intuition, self-confidence, etc. To be physically, mentally, and emotionally healthy, energy must be able to flow freely between chakras. These chakras, however, can be blocked by stress, lack of exercise, a poor diet, or an excess of negative thoughts. When this happens, the free movement of one's energy is obstructed and*

physical, emotional, and mental issues can arise. Yogic postures and breath exercises, therefore, are recommended to help unblock chakras, thereby bringing balance to one's overall well-being.[2]

I first heard about chakras through my good friend who is also a spiritual healer. She was the person who really made me understand the power of chakras and what happens when your chakras are closed. She wasn't forcing me to believe in it but more about being open to the possibility of certain chakras in my body stopping me from moving forward in my life.

She was great at opening my chakras, and this is coming from a person who thought this was all mumbo jumbo. At that point in my life, I had nothing to lose, so I tried it. Maybe there was something that my friend could see that I couldn't.

She explained that we have seven main chakras that operate in our bodies that we have to open so that we can achieve our highest version of ourself. When one chakra is closed, that can affect how we operate in your daily life. When my friend did a spiritual cleanse, she mentioned two chakras I had to work on that made so much sense.

I had to work on people pleasing and being grounded. Sometimes when you are lost and not sure what to do, you have to get to the basics. At the time, when my friend talked about chakras, I had no clue which chakra was which, so don't feel bad if you don't have a clue either. I will be sharing the seven main chakras and what they are.[3]

1. Root Chakra (Muladhara). The Root Chakra is located in the base of your spine. It is associated with the color red and is an earth element. The Root Chakra deals with feeling grounded and secure. When this chakra is closed, you don't feel secure about yourself, and therefore you won't have the confidence to move forward.

I believe in having a steady foundation; this whole book is about building the foundation of leadership. When you are not grounded and are feeling unstable, you lack clarity and confidence to move forward in your life. You are not sure of yourself because of the insecurities that were put on you by society and your culture.

This was one of the chakras that was closed off for me. I always feared the unknown and thought I wasn't good enough to create the life I desire. My foundation was unstable because there were so many thoughts I kept to myself and never had an outlet to share it them. Also at the time, I was afraid of how I was going to make money for myself, which is what happens when the root chakra is closed off.

All of this really stemmed from how I was brought up to do what I was told and never rock the boat or forge my own path.

2. Sacral Chakra (Swadhisthana). The Sacral Chakra is located at the bottom of the belly button. It is associated with the color orange and is a water element. This chakra deals with creativity and sexual energy. When this chakra is blocked, you feel like you have no control in your life.

3. Solar Plexus Chakra (Manipura). The Solar Plexus Chakra is located in the abdomen area. It is associated with the color yellow and is a fire element. This chakra deals with being able to be confident and express your true self. When this chakra is blocked, you have self-doubt and are unable to fully accept or love yourself.

This is also the chakra of people pleasing. As someone who is a people pleaser and a pushover, this was another chakra that was blocked for me. I was always worried about what others thought of me or what would happen if someone didn't like me. For years, I did what I was told to do in order to be liked. When you constantly keep doing things to please others, you lose your sense of self in the process.

4. Heart Chakra (Anahata). The Heart Chakra is located in the center of the chest, just above the heart. It is associated with the color green and is an air element. This chakra deals with being able to give and receive love from yourself and others. When this chakra is blocked, you will have a difficult time being able to open up to others and receive the love you deserve.

5. Throat Chakra (Vishuddha). The Throat Chakra is of course located in the throat. It is associated with the color light blue or turquoise and is a sound element. This chakra deals with your voice and being able to communicate your personal power. If this chakra gets blocked, it will be difficult for you to communicate how you feel.

6. Third-Eye Chakra (Ajna). The Third-Eye Chakra is located in the forehead in between your eyes. It is associated with the color dark blue or purple and is a light element. This chakra deals with being able to deal with the bigger picture and your intuition. When this chakra is blocked, it becomes challenging for you to dig deeper and trust your gut feeling.

7. Crown Chakra (Samsara or Sahasrara). The Crown Chakra is the highest chakra out of the seven and is located at the top of the head. It is associated with the color violet and is our divine consciousness. This is where you can connect with your highest self and your purpose in life.

How do traumas and chakras connect with each other? When you don't heal your traumas, then certain chakras are closed, which means you are blocking energy to heal from your traumas. You are keeping in negative energy instead of letting it out, and this also prevents you from welcoming in new energy to become the best version of yourself.

Instead of being the light, you are stuck in this dark place and feel like you cannot come out of it because of certain belief systems that are stopping you from moving forward.

Being able to open your chakras one by one enables you to focus on healing the kind of traumas you go through.

For me, when I was able to unblock the first and third chakra, I was able to let go of what others thought of me. Instead of fearing the unknown, I was able to embrace it. I was able to forge my own path regardless of the roadblocks that came my way.

Take Care of Your Mental Well-being

Mental health is another huge taboo in the Asian culture. In fact, it's a taboo in many cultures. When it comes to mental health, the Asian culture has always seen it as an illness. You never like to talk about it because if you do, you are deemed as "crazy."

Instead of finding ways to take care of your mental well-being, you are told to hide it. Your elders never want to deal with it or they think it's not real. Instead of being able to create a safe space to talk about how you feel, your elders do one of the extremes: ignore the problem thinking it will go away or put you in a mental institution so that they don't have to deal with it.

Your traumas can affect your mental health. If you constantly ignore them, that is how you end up feeling depressed, have major anxiety, and feel like you are not worthy. Since the pandemic, the topic of mental health has been more accepted than before because, let's face it, every single person went through some form of mental health challenge while being on lockdown. This was all brand-new to you without knowing what would happen, so of course this would affect your mental health.

The pandemic made you more fearful and paranoid. Everyday seemed like all you ever hear was bad news about the pandemic. You were afraid to see your friends or family thinking they might be a carrier, and not being able to go out in the beginning of the lockdown made it feel like you were trapped in your own home. It's even worse for women who had to homeschool their children, run the household, take care of family members, and still work a job or business. You felt so burnt out from all of it because you're in the constant mode of taking care of everyone else expect yourself.

It was even worse when you work from home. When companies had to pivot from closing their offices to having employees work from home, the stress grew for so many employees. Companies expected more output from you since you didn't have to travel to the office. Your office hours became all hours of the day for your clients and coworkers because you worked from home. When you have to share the internet with five other people in the house during the lockdown, the connection wasn't always the best so you ended up spending more time on your job at home than when you were in the office.

Not only did you face the mental health challenges of the pandemic, but you also had to deal with the racist attacks that you constantly saw in the news. It was worse for Asian women since we were targeted more than men, so, of course, all of this negatively affected your mental health.

A survey from MetroPlusHealth shares the current reality of mental health issues of Asian women in New York City. Here are the facts:

- Sixty-nine percent of Asian American women reported feeling comfortable talking to their doctor about their mental health compared to 80% of women in the general population.
- Seventy-two percent of Asian women reported having higher stress compared to 58% of the general population.
- Sixty-four percent of Asian women reported that the pandemic had a negative effect on their mental health compared to 40% of the general population.[4]

Your mental health should not be ignored at all. You have to learn to constantly take care of your mental well-being.

I remember when my best friend mentioned to me that her sister's car broke down because she never had the time to take the car to the dealer to get an oil change. Instead of bringing her car in to get the oil change when suggested, she just ignored it, thinking it was still okay to drive the car. Yes, for a period of time, it will work, but there will be a breaking point when the car will break down without proper care, and it will cost more to repair the problem.

Your mental health is the same. If you don't take proper care of it, you will break down. It's so important to talk about mental health and normalize it in the Asian community. I want the community, especially the women, to realize that they are not alone in these challenging times.

There are different ways you can take care of your mental well-being. You can seek a licensed mental health therapist, hire a coach, talk to your friends and family, or start a new hobby.

Sometimes you just need an outlet to clear your head and mind dump all your thoughts. You can do that through journaling, meditation, or working out. One of the things I did to mind dump and clear my head is jogging outside. I can tell when my mental health starts to creep up on me, when I haven't gone out for a jog in a long time. Once I start jogging, I feel like my mind has been cleared from all the disturbing thoughts in my head, and I am ready to seize the day. Sometimes I will listen to music while I jog, usually K-pop, or I just like to check out my surroundings.

Most of the time I like jogging to the beach that is close to where I live. There's something magical for me when I am around water. I just feel at peace, and it reminds me that no matter what I go through in life, I know everything will be okay. I usually jog for 30 minutes one way, walk around a bit, and jog back home. Jogging was another saving grace for me during the lockdown.

Another thing that I did during the pandemic was utilizing social media to create a safe space for our community to share our mental health challenges. Back when Clubhouse just started, it was a great social media app to connect with the world during the lockdowns. I would create chats where any woman could join and just talk about their mental health.

Many of the women felt at peace being able to share their fears and their thoughts. I learned a lot of things as well from the women who attended these chats, especially from women who lived outside of the United States and Canada.

I remember chatting with an Asian woman who lived in China, and she mentioned how China treats its women like garbage. But when she heard about the racist attacks in the United States and Canada, she mentioned that their situation in China was better than what we were dealing with. Isn't that sad that being treated like garbage was a better choice than being attacked in a hate crime. Both are bad!

I chatted with another Asian woman from Europe who mentioned that racist attacks were also prevalent in Europe, especially in France. She said France was a hotbed for anti-Asian hate crimes, which was shocking to me. When you live in countries like Canada and the United States, you tend to live in a bubble and forget what is happening to the rest of the world. It opened my eyes knowing we were not the only ones who were suffering.

K-dramas

This may be not typical, but I started watching massive amounts of K-dramas during the pandemic. The first K-drama I watched was *Crash Landing on You* and from then on, I was hooked on watching more.

The more I watched K-dramas, the more it was a healing process for me. These dramas had storylines that I could totally relate to even though I wasn't Korean. Each K-drama always created a backstory of the characters and the traumas they faced in the past that led them to their current situation. Being able to see their backstory made me understand why they were in the state that they were in. It made me feel like I wasn't the only person going through the challenges I went through.

Watching K-dramas also was an escape from the constant bad news that surrounded the pandemic. Being able to escape from reality, even if it was for a little bit, gave some comfort in my mental health during the pandemic.

In 12–16 episodes, you were able to watch situations that you could apply in real life. Whether it was someone dealing with death or being bullied by their peers, you could relate to how that made you feel and could see the negative effects of it if you didn't go through the healing process.

Here are three K-dramas to watch that are great to learn about healing from your traumas.

Move to Heaven

This K-drama totally made me cry buckets of tears. *Move to Heaven* is a story about a boy who suffers from Asperger syndrome and suddenly loses his father due to a heart condition. Now he is under the care of his ex-convict uncle, who helps him run their trauma cleaning business. What I really loved about this show was how each time they went to clean a house from a death scene, they were able to uncover the story of the deceased person by collecting certain items during their cleaning, putting them in a yellow box, and giving it to the next of kin. Being able to uncover this story shows you how you deal with death of a loved one and how you can heal from grief, which is never easy.

Sky Castle

This is a show most Asian families can relate to. The show is about affluent families living in a prestigious neighborhood in South Korea and the pressure to always be the best in everything. You see the children in this neighborhood being constantly pressured by their parents to study nonstop so they can get into the best schools to the point where they are willing to cheat and bring others down just to get to the top. In this show, you see the children break down and go through so many mental health challenges, such as through depression and anxiety, because of this pressure to be the best. In the end, the parents realize how their actions affect their children and decide to stop obsessing to get them into the top schools.

It's Okay Not to Be Okay

This show is definitely a must watch. It shows different types of mental illness that people go through, such as battling antisocial personality disorder. It also shows how a childhood traumatic experience can linger onto your adult life if you don't go through the proper ways to heal from it and how being able to lean on others can help you heal your traumas in the process. The storyline is a little bit complicated to explain so it's definitely better to watch it and see for yourself.

I could definitely suggest more K-dramas, but this would become a super long chapter. Plus, I have a good friend who has been able to create a platform where she utilizes K-dramas to promote mental health. You can check out *Noona's Noonchi*, where Jeanie Chang, who is also a licensed marriage and family therapist, creates videos, interviews, and reels talking about K-dramas from a mental health perspective. I was fortunate to be one of her guest on her podcast.[5]

Seek Professional Help

It's very important to seek help to heal from your traumas. Being able to seek help shouldn't be seen as something shameful or a handout. This has to be seen as part of your healing process because you can learn to heal faster this way.

Trying to do this on your own will be challenging since you have blind spots. These blind spots are holding you back from healing. There are many ways to seek help to heal from your traumas.

You can talk to a licensed therapist who is knowledgeable in this field and can help you work through your process. Be okay with seeking professional help. I know it's easier said than done because you have been conditioned to think something is wrong with you when you seek professional help. You have to ask yourself what is more important, worrying about what others think or being able to heal from your traumas.

Seeking help doesn't always have to mean seeking professional help as well. Remember, do what works for you. Sometimes it can be simple as listening to a podcast, reading a book, or joining a support group. The main point of this is that you are not in your journey alone.

Remember in the last chapter when I mentioned I was going through depression, anxiety, and paranoia during the lockdowns? If my family hadn't been there for me to help me cry it out or talk about it, I wouldn't be where I am today.

Of course it wasn't pretty when that happened. There was a lot of screaming during this difficult time, but the most important thing was that we were able to sit down and talk about what we were feeling in that moment and the pent-up anger we had for each other. This was something that we never did as a family. Most of the time, we just kept it to ourselves and never confronted each other because by not saying anything meant the problem would go away.

Being able to go through this process gave me permission to share my feelings and not have to be ashamed about it. I am more open about how I am feeling and what I fear now. It's refreshing to be able to say things out loud and not have to be embarrassed about what I feel. There is no reason to be embarrassed about feelings to begin with. We are all human beings, and we will go through good and bad days. The difference is that when times get tough, being able to have some kind of support system can go a long way.

I am blessed to have different support systems in my life. I have my family, my friends, and women in business that I can confide in. When you become an entrepreneur, it can be a lonely journey, and sometimes you need to be surrounded with like-minded people who get what you are going through.

I have been able to share some of the ways to start healing from traumas, and I left the best one for last, which is the journey to self-love and why it matters, which I will discuss in the next chapter.

6

The Journey to Self-Love

SELF-LOVE IS SOMETHING that you are not taught by society or your culture. As a woman, you have been taught to take care of everyone else, and because you have been programmed to always think of others first, you forget to take care of yourself.

I wish self-love was taught in schools as well so that the future generations will not go through the low self-esteem issues that we face today. While it's great that schools teach math and science, self-love and self-development are just as important.

If self-love were taught in my school, I know I would be a lot kinder to myself instead of being my worst enemy. I would stop criticizing myself and worry less about what other people thought of me. But everything happens for a reason, and I always believe the situations that happens in our life are either a blessing or a lesson.

To be honest, I only started loving my true self in my 30s. I really learned true self-love while living in Hawaii for two winters. This was a time where I was really learning to love my own company and realized what I would and would not tolerate. It was also a time of learning to heal for myself.

At the time, I had no real idea why I decided to go to Hawaii. One very cold winter night in Toronto, and I mean very cold, I started thinking that I wanted to live somewhere outside of Canada, and Hawaii just popped up on my computer screen. Since then, I was obsessed with going to Hawaii. I did everything in my power to go there and just made it happen.

Many people thought I was unusual because I did things that were totally not typical, especially as an Asian woman. I decided to sell my condo when my mortgage was up for renewal. I quit my job of 12 years (and my parents were livid when that happened) and sold everything I owned.

The first time I set foot in Hawaii was in the summer of 2014. I went with my two best friends and my goddaughter. The moment I landed in Hawaii, I could totally feel the energy it was giving me and for 10 days, I had the best time. It felt so great that I decided to go back in November of the same year and lived there for 6 months.

It was one of the greatest moments of my life. I was by myself living the island life not knowing what was going to happen. I had my worries, of course. This was the first time in my life when I had no plan of what to do; I was constantly freaking out if I was going to make it or not. Even though I had my worries, I still went out and lived my life. I met some great people along the way and did many things that I previously would never have done by myself.

I would eat at restaurants by myself, go to the beach by myself, and explore the city by myself. This was not typical of me because I always felt awkward doing things by myself because I thought people would laugh at me or find me weird that I was out and about on my own. It was also hard to learn to enjoy my own company since it was something new.

The more I did enjoy my own company, the more I learned to love myself completely. There were also people along the way who helped me learn to love myself as well. I was able to meet amazing people while staying in Hawaii. Going to Hawaii was my form of healing, and even though I was going through a lot of things in my life, at least I was able to do this in paradise.

I actually went back to Hawaii again the next winter to live for another 6 months, and it allowed me to be open to new things whether they were good or bad. I went through different things that I never thought was possible if I didn't decide to listen to my heart. I will forever be grateful for my times in Hawaii. There is an energy there that is amazing, and you will understand it more the moment you set foot in it. Hawaii goes beyond just beaches and palm trees, even though that was a bonus.

Before that, I was always pleasing others and never saw my own worth. I would let people walk all over me, constantly seek approval, and just do whatever society tells me to do. Any imperfections I had, I hated it because I also wanted to attain perfection.

All this led me to having low self-confidence and being too afraid to set out my own path. It was the main reason why I started my podcast, *The Tao of Self-Confidence*. Back in 2015, I was looking for support systems that catered to helping Asian women with their self-confidence, and to my surprise there weren't any.

For the longest time I thought I was the only person who dealt with confidence issues and everyone else was fine. I also realized that it was not typical for the Asian culture to talk about the negative emotions and issues that come up in life. So I decided to start the podcast as a support system and as a way to create a stronger representation of Asian women, because at the time, it was so needed.

While interviewing many Asian women on the topic of self-confidence, I realized that the moment they started loving themselves completely was the moment they start to believe in themselves and forge their own path. Each woman had her own way of self-love, and it was great to learn from these amazing women.

For the longest time, I always thought self-love was only loving the good parts of me, and I attracted the same things in life. I attracted the people who only accepted the good parts of me, and because of that I never showed up as my true self. I thought I always had to be the perfect person to my friends, family, past boyfriends, and business.

I was always afraid to show my weaknesses and imperfections. I thought if I showed that side of me, people would not accept me, so I hid that side of me. I felt trapped in myself, not being able to show up as my authentic self because of my constant seeking of approval from everyone.

It took me a while to realize that what I thought was self-love was the total opposite. It was actually self-sabotage. I would constantly get mad at myself if I made a mistake or if I looked in the mirror and I saw my love handles were hanging out of my pants. I became my own worst enemy and was constantly my own mean girl instead of being my own best friend.

And when you think about it, you would never be mean to your own best friend. If your best friend was going through something or feeling down on herself, you would be her biggest cheerleader, right? So why can't you be the same for yourself?

Learning to love all parts of yourself takes work on your part as well because not only are you learning something new, you also have to unlearn a lot of things you picked up from the moment you were born. You have to unpack a lot things that are stopping you from loving yourself, such as your traumas and perceptions of yourself.

And if you don't unpack these impediments you are stuck in the same cycle, thinking you are never good enough and that you have to show up a certain way. That is not the way to live. This is why learning to love yourself is so important in your journey. In order to be the leader you wish to be, it starts with self-love and that means to love all parts of yourself, even if it means you have a pimple that is the size of Mount Rushmore.

Being able to fully love yourself (the good, the bad, and the ugly) is what is needed to be the leader that you are meant to be because being a leader isn't about perfection; it's about going out there and showing others what is possible. Your journey will never be perfect, you will have mistakes and failures along the way, but when you can love yourself enough to keep moving forward, imagine the positive impact that you will create for yourself and for our current and future generations.

Be okay with making mistakes, be okay with being vulnerable, and accept your imperfections and weaknesses while showing your strengths. This is what truly makes you the beautiful and imperfect self that you are meant to be. Leadership is about learning from your mistakes, being able to fail forward, and being okay to show your vulnerable side.

Self-love is essential for every single person. You have to learn to love yourself first and foremost in order to know the kind of love you deserve from others. I do believe that how you love yourself is how others will love you because it is what you are attracting into your life.

For me that's what happened. I always attracted men who loved only the good parts of me so I was never able to show up as my true self. I was always constantly seeking approval, making sure I was good enough for the opposite sex. I was always afraid they were going to leave me, so I never wanted to rock the boat as well. I did everything and anything to avoid fights because I thought if I had a fight with my boyfriend at the time, it was a sign that the relationship was over. Everything I did, I always wanted to make sure that I was the perfect girlfriend with no troubles at all, but of course that is unattainable.

I also thought that I had to always be a positive person and never show any negative emotions. There is nothing wrong with being positive, of course, but there is also such a thing as toxic positivity. That was me, Miss Always Positive, even though on the inside I was dealing with all kinds of crap. When you keep your negative emotions in and have no way to let it out, it can destroy you. There would be times where I would just start crying for no reason, and I realized it was because I just needed to let out everything that I was feeling, even if I didn't know it at the time.

The Asian culture constantly tells you to make everyone else happy, putting everyone else's needs ahead of your own, and you end up neglecting the most important person in the world, which is yourself. You feel like in order to be loved by others you constantly have to attend to their every need. This can become toxic for you, and this is why you end up being taken advantage of and not be taken seriously in anything that you do. You think what you are doing is a good thing when it's not.

I remember watching *Partner Track* on Netflix, and there was one scene in the show where Ingrid Yun, the main character, told her parents that she didn't make partner in her law firm and decided to quit her job. Ingrid's father wanted her to apologize to the firm and beg for her job back, which she wasn't happy about. That scene made me feel for her. If you watched the show, then you know what I am talking about. If you haven't seen the show, there will be spoilers.

The truth is, no matter what Ingrid did, she was never going to make partner in her law firm. She gave six years of her life to show her colleagues and boss that she had what it takes to be partner at the law firm she was working for. She worked all hours of the night, dedicated her life to her job, she did everything her boss told her to do, even if it meant throwing her friends under the bus. She did all of these to show her boss she was capable of becoming partner, but in the end she never got it, and she knew she was never going to get it because she was female, and even more so, she was an Asian female lawyer whom nobody took seriously. The firm used her to get the job done and gave her false promises of potentially becoming partner at the law firm.

I was like Ingrid at my old job. I did exactly the same thing. I would always be the first person to come in the office and the last person to leave. I dedicated my whole life to my job, and there were years where I didn't even take a vacation because I was so afraid that if I took vacation, I might end up getting a permanent vacation. In the end, I realized my boss never took me seriously because he would tell everyone else that my job was easy and that any person could do what I was doing. Of course, I felt small thinking that all my efforts were not appreciated. So I totally get how Ingrid was feeling, and watching those scenes was something I could relate to.

In fact, I know many female lawyers can relate to Ingrid's situation where they did everything they could to make partner and never got it because of their gender. It's not easy to be the only woman in a white-male dominated industry. Even if you did make partner, it wasn't like you made it. In fact, I remember talking to an Asian female lawyer who did make partner, and she still went through hell. Her male partners would constantly harass and threaten her because they thought she shouldn't have made partner, and this happened about a year ago.

The pandemic also made women feel more burnt out than ever, especially during the lockdown. You had to work a job or run your business, run the household, take care of the kids, homeschool your kids, run errands, and also take care of your other family members. Doing all this at once can of course take a toll on you. Also working from home may sound great, but for women, it came with more pressure than being in the office. Most companies thought that if you were working from home, you'd have more working hours to get the job done. You'd have clients calling you all hours of the night because of it, and when your internet connection at home wasn't as strong as the internet connection in the office, it slowed down everything. Your 8-hour shift became a 12-hour shift or more.

A study from Deloitte called *Women at Work 2022: A Global Outlook* was aimed at understanding women's experience in the workplace during the pandemic. They surveyed 5,000 women in 10 countries and this is what they found:

- Fifty-three percent of the women who were surveyed reported higher stress levels than the previous year.
- Forty-six percent of the women reported feeling burnt out.
- Fifty-nine percent of the women experienced harassment or micro-aggressions over the previous year.
- As hybrid work became the new norm, almost 60% of the women who work in this environment reported feeling excluded from important meetings and that they didn't have the exposure needed for career progression.
- Forty-two percent of the women worried that their career progression would be affected if they were not constantly available.[1]

Self-care Is Essential

During the pandemic years of 2020 and into 2021, there was a 250% increase in self-care related searches on Google.[2] When the whole world was on lockdown, of course many things affected you, especially your mental health, and you had to find ways to take care of yourself during that time. Self-care is part of the act of self-love, yet sometimes it's hard for you to even give yourself five minutes of ME time because you are always on the go, especially women.

I have learned to always set aside time for self-care. Whether it's watching a YouTube video or even just walking outside, this is time that I aside for myself to rest and recharge so I don't get stressed or burned out.

There are so many ways for you to practice self-care. You just have to choose what works for you. It doesn't have to be anything too out of the ordinary. In fact, it can be something as simple as washing the dishes. For me, it's quite therapeutic when I am washing the dishes, which is the only reason why I mentioned that. It could also mean having a day at the salon to pamper yourself or even a shopping spree. Again the main point of this is that you have a self-care routine to step away from everything. It's necessary to create that ME time.

Here's some other ways you can practice self-care:

- Listen to music.
- Exercise or move around for 30 minutes.
- Read a book.
- Listen to podcasts.
- Take a nap.
- Carve out some time to meditate.
- Try something new.
- Take a social media detox.
- Journal your thoughts.
- Have a spa day.
- Have a girls day or night out.
- Get a mani-pedi for yourself.

This list can go on, but this is a great start to your self-care journey. You can also create a self-care routine by setting 15 minutes aside for yourself. You can do this first thing in the morning or late at night or even both. Having that routine can help you with practicing self-care a lot better.

These activities are so simple, yet you feel guilty at times when you choose to have time set aside for yourself. There is no shame in practicing self-care. It is needed in your daily life, and it's time you start creating a self-care practice that works for you.

There is a difference between self-care and self-love. Self-care is what you do to take care of yourself, whether it's physically, mentally, spiritually, or emotionally. Self-love is learning to love yourself including your flaws. It's about fully accepting yourself with your imperfections. The next section will give you different self-love practices that you can use for yourself.[3]

Self-Love Practices

Here's some of the self-love practices that have helped me in my own journey. I hope these can help you as well.

Affirmations

As cheesy as this sounds, having affirmations is a great way to practice self-love. Most people think you need to say 101 affirmations to make it work. You can choose to have 101 affirmations, but I just say three affirmations to myself when I am having moments of self-doubt. These are my affirmations:

I am loved.

I am enough.

I am worthy.

That's it. I keep it super simple. Of course when you start saying this to yourself for the first time, it's going to feel weird and awkward. It's normal to feel that way when you start something new. It was the same for me when I started saying this to myself, but the more you keep saying these affirmations, the less awkward you will feel. Also, in the beginning, you might not believe in the affirmations as you are saying them. That's okay; just keep saying them until you can believe that they are true. Nothing happens overnight.

Loving Mirror Exercise

This was probably one of the best exercises I did for myself. I first heard about this exercise through a women's group that I was part of. To be honest, it was really uncomfortable for me to even do this exercise, but I'm glad I was able to get out of my own way to make this happen.

What you are supposed to do is ask someone close to you five or six simple questions about yourself. This person can be your best friend, a family member, or your partner. Really anybody who really knows you very well. The person you choose to take part in this exercise can either send you a video or written reply answering the questions you sent. You should make answering the questions comfortable for the other person because not everyone is comfortable with video.

I asked my best friend to do the loving mirror exercise with me, and she sent her answers through email. I will share with you the questions you can ask the person you choose to do this exercise with, and the answers my best friend sent me.

Question 1—What do you get out of me being in your life?

A better me! Your unwavering support and encouragement makes me a better person; you take me as I am and want nothing but the best for me. You show this by encouraging and motivating me whenever I want to give up, allowing me to be the best person I can be. You provide me with the needed boost of confidence to my self-esteem those times when I'm down and think I can't do something. And last but not least, your constant friendship and loyalty provides a much welcomed and needed comfort in my life, with the knowledge there is someone I can always rely on for anything.

Question 2—What have you gained from our relationship? (Be specific.)

Personal growth— You try to live your life to the fullest and are not afraid to try new things. I am more reserved and laid back but by you sharing and talking about your experiences, I find myself living vicariously through you, which, in turn, allows me to learn and experience things I may not have thought about doing.

A more positive outlook in life—You surround yourself with positivity, from the way you live your life (i.e., live a more healthy lifestyle, cut out the negative/bad habits in your life, etc.) to your outlook in life (your optimism); which in turn makes me try to live my life the same way.

Question 3—What would be missing if I weren't in your life?

My life would definitely be a lot lonelier. But to be honest, I honestly can't imagine what it would be like if you weren't in my life. I rely and depend on you on a lot of things—from the smallest matter of knowing you're there to listen when I'm mad and need an ear to vent to knowing I have your shoulder to cry on when times are tough.

Question 4—What do you see as my strengths?,

In no specific order, your loyalty (knowing I can always count you for anything), honesty (you will always tell me the truth, no matter how harsh it is), your sense of humor (you have the ability to make anyone smile and laugh with your jokes, no matter how corny they are), and your outgoing personality (you make it comfortable to be in new surroundings with your personality).

Question 5—On a scale of 1–10, what would you rate our relationship?

10+

Questions 6—(If anything less than a 10) What can I do to make it a 10?

When I first read my best friend's responses to this exercise, I was bawling my eyes out because I had no idea this is what she thought of me. This is something I go back to when I am feeling down on myself. I go back to reading this and knowing that there's someone in my corner who sees so much good and potential that I am not always able to see.

I highly recommend doing this exercise for yourself. This really can change your outlook about yourself and can help you learn to love yourself more.

Give Yourself Permission

I think this is very important when it comes to loving yourself. So often you have been seeking permission or approval from others, especially when you decide to forge your own path. Constantly seeking this permission delays your own success, and you feel like you are not good enough to go out and make things happen.

I want you to realize that the only person you need permission from is yourself. When you realize this, you open yourself to so many opportunities you never thought were possible.

Even writing this book, I had so many things running through my brain. I was going through major imposter syndrome thinking I wasn't good enough to write this book. I was thinking, "What gave me the right to be the person to write a book about leadership?"

I went through so many limiting thoughts in my head because of how I was brought up, but the moment I said to myself that I can make this happen and the only person I needed permission from was me, the rest was history. Writing this book wasn't only for me; this book is for you as well, to show you what is possible and let you know that you are never alone in this journey.

Stop waiting or seeking permission from others to start a new journey. Just make it happen, and your future self will thank you for it.

Become Your Own Best Friend

I mentioned this earlier in this chapter, but I wanted to make sure this was included again because you can be your own worst enemy. Myself included. Back then, I was so hard on myself. If I made a mistake, I would put myself down and call myself a failure.

Every time you are mean to yourself, just think of how you would treat your own best friend. If your best friend was having a rough time or feeling down on herself, would you treat her the same as how you would treat yourself? Of course not!

Start being kinder to yourself when you make mistakes, become your biggest cheerleader, advocate for yourself, and celebrate your own wins. The most important relationship you can work on is the relationship with yourself. What you say to yourself matters because if you are constantly saying negative things about yourself, then you can never move forward and be the leader that you were meant to be. When you are able to become your own best friend, everything else will fall into place.

Set Boundaries

How many times in your life have you said YES when someone asked you to do something? Whether it's your parents, friends, or work colleagues, you can't just say NO, even though deep inside you want to.

I have been there as well. When you grow up in a culture where you are do as you're told, it's hard to say NO to the things that don't serve you. You constantly feel like you always have to say YES or else you will be seen as difficult or you don't want to be less liked by people.

You constantly say YES to the point where people walk all over you or you are taken for granted because you are too nice and never want to say NO to avoid conflict. You feel less of a person if you say NO, and you get the biggest guilt trip in the process.

This is why it's so important to set boundaries for yourself. Learn to say NO to the things that don't serve you or that you don't want to do. If a person makes you feel guilty and says something mean because you said NO, they are not your people.

The real people will understand and respect your decision and move on. Being able to set boundaries allows you to do things you want to do or say YES to the opportunities that are meant for you. Being able to set boundaries, you will be able to show up as your true self, and you will also be able to find peace with yourself.

Let Go of What Others Say About You

You may have heard this many times before, but it's really important for you to learn to let go of what others say about you. As someone who comes from a culture in which I get nonstop comments about my appearance, my marital status, and my career, I know it can be challenging.

It took a lot of work on myself to realize that what others may say about me are not the absolute truth and that they are just someone's opinions, but it's hard when that is all you know, and you think that is your absolute truth.

There were many times where I was told I was fat, or to stop eating or I would get fat. There were times where all of my Asian aunties would ask me when I would get married or hand me a prayer book so that I could pray for a husband. There were also times when people asked me when I was going to get a job and take my life seriously, even though the path that I was taking was a serious path. All of this can definitely bring down a person's worth and confidence when you are bombarded with nonstop comments from your peers, especially when they're family.

Of course, there comes a time where you will learn to care less about what others say about you and focus on yourself and what you are meant to do. The more you work on loving yourself and knowing your purpose, the less everything else will matter. It may take time on your part because there are so many things you have to unlearn, but you will get there.

Also, there is something you may have to realize, especially when it comes to the Asian culture. Our aunties and uncles who make comments that are offensive to us are just saying what they are thinking. While to them there is no malice, to you it can be hurtful, and it's hard sometimes to tell them that their words hurt because they don't understand the implications of their actions. I know this isn't right, but I hope this also helps you realize to not take their words too seriously. Of course not every Asian aunty or uncle is like that, but most of them just say what they are thinking.

When I realized this, it helped me learn to not take their words so seriously. Do I still get random comments from my aunties and uncles? Of course I do. Do I take offense? No, instead I just laugh it off and keep doing my thing, and I still get similar comments from them until this day. How you react to it is what matters the most.

So even though it may seem impossible or lots of efforts on your part, do the work because you will feel so much better about yourself when you are able to let go of what anyone says to you. Know that not everybody will like you and there will be some people who will say mean things about you; that's just life. You can let it get to you or you can brush it off and know that you are more than enough to be the person and leader you are meant to be.

Ask for Help and/or Support

Just remember that anything you do in life you don't have to be alone. You may be in this journey of self-love for yourself, but you never have to be in this journey by yourself. Love yourself enough to ask for help.

The loving mirror exercise was an exercise that I did with my best friend. I wouldn't have been able to receive the aha moments that I got if I didn't reach out to her to do this exercise with me. There are so many ways to ask for help or support. You can hire a coach, have an accountability partner, or you can join a community or group who will help you learn to love yourself.

All of this is critical in your journey because when you try to do things on your own, you have a lot of blind spots that prevent you from becoming your best self. This is why having help and support is needed. The help and support you seek can see what you can't see and change the way you see things.

There are many great resources that you can check out online to help you with your journey to self-love. You can read self-help books, listen to podcasts, or watch YouTube videos. In the end, you choose what works for you.

I have been fortunate to have a circle of friends whom I can turn to when I need help or when I am having moments of self-doubt. I can turn to them, and they help me come out of my funk or pump me up to keep moving forward. Little things like this can go a long way in your journey.

A Study on Self-Love

There are positive and negative effects when women have high and low indexes of self-love. The Body Shop interviewed 22,000 people ages 18 and older on the topic of self-love in December 2020. They created a report called the Global Self-Love Index. The report showed the different facets of self-love, such as emotions, social media, perception, and more. Here's some of the facts that The Body Shop were able to find during this report.

- The countries with the lowest self-love index were South Korea, France, Saudi Arabia, China, and Spain.
- The countries with the highest self-love index were Denmark, Australia, United States, South Africa, and Mexico.
- One in two people feel more self-doubt than self-love
- Six in 10 people around the world wish they had more self-respect for themselves.
- Women with low self-love are five times more likely to say that they rely on what others think of them.
- Self-doubt affects women more than men: 64% of women feel more anxious and nervous compared to 58% of men, 57% of women feel more depressed compared to 50% of men, and 60% of women feel that they are not able to stop worrying compared to 53% of men.
- Globally, people who use social media influencers, celebrities, and models in advertisements are the biggest contributors to low levels of self-esteem.
- Globally, older people have more love for themselves than the younger generation, especially Gen Z who experience the lowest score for self-love.
- The beauty industry is also a major contributor to low self-love, especially when photos are photoshopped or airbrushed to give an unattainable perception of beauty, while lack of diversity is also another factor.[4]

These facts show that many factors contribute to your journey of self-love and they can affect you in all parts of your life. This is why your journey to self-love matters more than you realize.

Being able to love yourself fully is what will help you build resilience, build confidence, have a better relationship with yourself and others, overcome the many fears you face, and most importantly, you start believing in yourself and your abilities to move forward to be the leader that you are meant to be.

Of course this work is never easy. You have to unlearn many things and go through the healing process, which can be ugly and painful, but when you can get to the other side, magic happens, and you become the person that you have been longing for all your life.

You are probably wondering, how do you even begin this journey of self-love? What do you have to do to start being the person you want to be. It really starts with building confidence, which will be the next chapter. Confidence is something that I have been talking about for the last 7 years, ever since I started my podcast, and without it, I wouldn't be here today sharing my story and what I have learned to pass on to you.

7

The Power of Self-Confidence

Self-confidence is what will help you become the person who you are meant to be. It will propel you to take action, be the change you want to see in the world, know your worth, become courageous, and realize your potential. That's what self-confidence has done for me. Without it, I wouldn't be here today sharing everything that I have learned in my journey. This path is never easy because, if it were, everyone would be doing it.

Building self-confidence takes daily work on your part. It's something that doesn't happen overnight. There are so many misconceptions when it comes to building your self-confidence, and I had my own as well.

I thought in order to be confident, you had to show up as loud and boisterous. I always thought there was only one way to build confidence, when it reality there are so many different ways to build your confidence. You can still be an introvert and be confident at the same time. The best part of this journey is that you get to choose what works for you.

This was the biggest lesson for me. I realize that everyone will have a different way of building confidence, and that is okay. In fact, it should be different because every person is different. It doesn't make sense that you only focus on one way of doing things because it will fall apart.

I will be sharing with you some of the things that I have done to build my own confidence. These may or may not work for you. I want to give you options that you can use to build your own self-confidence so you can be the leader that you are meant to be.

What Is Self-Confidence?

The first thing you need to start with is what is self-confidence? According to HealthyPlace:

> *Self-confidence, then, is the courage to know yourself, believe in yourself, and act on your beliefs. A definition of self-confidence is a positive feeling about oneself and the world that leads to courageous actions born out of a sense of self-respect.*[1]

As an Asian woman, having trust in yourself is not common, especially when you have been told all of your life how to live. From the moment you are born, you already have a plan laid out for you and anything outside of that path is considered shameful. Because you have been taught to live for others, it becomes a challenge to trust your own instincts, make your own decisions, and take action. Does this sound like you?

Don't worry because that was me as well. It was hard for me to make a decision for every single thing. I would never trust my instinct, and I would always overthink and second guess everything to the point that I never took action in what I wanted to do.

The fact that I had a podcast about self-confidence, I was the least confident. It was so hard for me to trust myself and because of it, I delayed my own success. I kept on comparing myself to all the wonderful women I have interviewed feeling small. This is not what I want for you. I want you to learn from my mistakes so that you don't have to spend 5–10 years thinking what if, when you can just take action and make things happen. It will not be perfect, and you will make mistakes along the way but imagine the impact you can create for yourself and for others.

That is why self-confidence is so important. You will be experiencing things that will be frustrating, and there will be days when you will struggle or be in a rut, but when you have the confidence to pick yourself back up and move forward, you become unstoppable.

Three Steps to Building Self-Confidence

I created a three-step process when it comes to building self-confidence. I think this three-step process can help anyone who is struggling to start their confidence journey.

Step 1—Believe in Yourself

This is the first and most important step because without it, you cannot move forward. You have to have this innate knowing in yourself that you can go out there and make things happen no matter what your circumstances are.

You don't have to know everything; you just have to know that when there's a will then there's a way.

Believing in yourself is the foundation of building self-confidence. If you don't have the right mindset to achieve your goals, you will not go out there and make things happen. This may sound cliché because you often hear this from everyone, but it is very critical. If you don't believe in yourself, you are delaying your own success.

Step 2—Educate Yourself

It's important to learn different ways to build your self-confidence. You have to see what methods will and will not work for you in your journey. As I mentioned, what may work for me might not work for you, and vice versa.

For me, I tried meditation as a way to build my self-confidence. Every time I would play a meditation audio on YouTube and start the process, I would totally fall asleep. I tried at least 10 more times, and it was the same outcome. For the longest time, I thought something was wrong with me because meditation didn't work for me. It took me a while to realize that this form of meditation wasn't meant for me. After having that realization, I felt so much better about myself and moved on to find different ways to build my confidence.

So be open to trying different ways to build confidence. Figure out what are the best methods for you, and when you can do it, it will make your journey easier and fun.

Step 3—Take Action

Taking action is necessary. Taking action is what leads you to the results and the opportunities you wish to see. Being able to take action in my own journey is what has helped me be the person that I am today.

The more you can take action, the more your confidence increases, and it will propel you to keep moving forward. You may not always take the right action, but it will lead you to the opportunities you deserve.

There were so many instances in my life where I would constantly take the wrong action thinking I was a failure, but in reality, I was on the right path because after looking back at the things I did, I realized the wrong actions I took had to happen.

I remember I would picture something in my head of how things should happen, and in real life, the total opposite happened. I thought I was a failure because it didn't happen how I pictured it. But now as I look back on that experience, I am glad it happened the way it did because it led me to this very moment.

Every action that you take, no matter how big or small it may be, it will lead you to taking more action. The more action you take, the more you can accomplish and the more confidence you will have in yourself and your capabilities.

The most important action you will take in your life is taking the first step of your journey. I know how scary that can be. You have all kinds of thoughts in your head; you constantly second-guess yourself, you keep going back with the will-you-or-won't-you thinking, and the first step or action that you take becomes such a big moment to overcome that it stops you from taking any action. *Do it anyway*. Your future self will thank you for it.

Bruce Lee once said, "I fear not the man who has practiced 10,000 kicks once, but I fear the man who has practiced one kick 10,000 times."

Take it one step or action at a time, and you will create the progress and confidence along the way.

Here's some of the self-confidence building methods I have used in my own journey.

Have a Purpose

It is important to have a purpose that is bigger than you. Having a purpose will give you the drive to take action. You are taking action not just for yourself but for the people you want to create a positive impact for. Your purpose doesn't have to fit everyone in the world. For some people, your purpose can be your children, and that is okay because this is something that most people can still relate to and you are still creating a huge impact in the world.

My purpose is to create a stronger representation for Asian women is what keeps me going no matter what the circumstances are. There are times where I feel like quitting, or I wonder if what I am doing makes sense.

Then I get a message from a podcast listener or a connection on LinkedIn, and they share with me that my content has helped them with their own confidence. Their messages are proof that I am in the right path. Even if I am in rut, which does happen because life is never linear, my purpose puts me back in the right direction.

In all honesty, the messages that I get from my podcast and from social media are what keeps me pumped up and going. They help me get excited about the possibilities for myself, for my community, and beyond. I have gotten messages from women who have been able to speak in public, start their own business, and share what they are going through. All of these are very important because this is something that you are not taught to do in your life, and it takes a lot of confidence and courage to do this. I get excited because I get to be part of these women's path to greatness.

Don't worry if you have no idea what your purpose is. It's okay if you don't know right now. You can work on it and fine-tune it the more you take action. Sometimes, your purpose will change because you are stepping into your element, so your thinking will change and your purpose will change in the process.

Face Your Fears

One of the biggest ways to build your confidence is to face your fears. I believe that being fearless doesn't mean you have no fears; it means you feel the fear and do it anyway. Every person on this earth fears something. Even leaders have fears, but the difference is that they face their fears head on. It's not easy, but it can give you the big boost of confidence knowing that you can overcome anything in life.

I have had my share of fears; whether it's in business or life, I had to overcome them in order to move forward. Every stage of my life, there was a fear that I had to face.

I remember doing my first YouTube video. Believe it or not, I was totally afraid of being on video. I would have major anxiety just thinking about putting myself out on video. I would put it off to the next day and the next day became 4 months later. Every time I would hit the record button, I would stop it right away. I was so afraid of how I looked on video, if people would laugh at me, or if people might think I was weird.

Back then, I was totally mortified by the thought of putting myself on video. I remember the first time I recorded my YouTube video. It was supposed to be a 2-minute video about how cool it was to work from home. The 2-minute video that I recorded turned into a 2-hour recording session. It felt embarrassing, I was stuttering like there was no tomorrow, my hands were super sweaty, and I had butterflies in my stomach. Even though I went through all of this, I was able to create my first video and share it with the world.

I started making more videos to get over that fear. The anxiety and fear I had from before started to show up less and I got better at being on video. In fact there was a whole month where I recorded three videos a day. Being able to do that helped get over my fear of video, and now I am comfortable being on video. I'm able to do video interviews, be on TV, and create my own videos. That wouldn't have happened if I didn't face my fear of being on video.

I also was asked to be a guest on CGTN, which is a huge TV network in China. When I said yes to the interview, I had no idea how big their audience was until I searched their Facebook page and saw they had more than 100 million followers. I also felt like I was going to have a heart attack when I saw that number and the fact that I was being interviewed on a prime time news channel with an award-winning host. Prime time means there are a lot of eyes tuning in. I was about to puke out of nervousness.

I still went ahead and did the interview. I couldn't turn back now. The good thing about this was that I wasn't the only person on the panel of interviewees, so for 30 minutes of live TV, it wasn't all me. The bad thing about this was when the host asked me a certain question and I literally blanked out on live, national television in China. If the host didn't have a follow-up question, I would've blanked out a lot longer. After that interview I realized I didn't die and if that is the worst thing that could happen to me on TV, then I can move forward.

When it comes to overcoming your fears, it may seem so big that you are too afraid to make the first step. I get it because I was like you. I would delay myself so many times because the fear took over me to the point that I resisted taking so much action in my life and delayed my own journey.

Once you make the decision to face your fears or take the first steps toward that, you will feel so proud of yourself, and you will continue to overcome any other fears that you may have.

One way that I was able to overcome my fears was to write down the possible outcomes when I decided to take action. An example would be, if I wanted to cold contact a person to buy a product or service from me, there were three possible outcomes. The person would say yes, no, or I would just get ghosted. If I was able to accept these possible outcomes, then I could move ahead with the decision.

The 51% Rule

I used to think that in order to be confident, you had to believe in yourself 100% of the time to start making moves. Then I learned about the 51% rule through an online group coaching program that I was part of.

This rule meant that you just needed to believe in yourself 51%. You are probably wondering why this specific number right? Because you needed a little bit more to believe in yourself than not believe in yourself, and 51% is the sweet spot. At 51%, you can start building that up to get to 100% if that is the goal.

I have applied this rule a lot in my life. I realize that 51% is the minimum that I strive for because I can build it up as I go. When I can get to 51% confidence, I build myself up and my confidence up at the same time.

What Is Your Confidence Color?

If you know me or have seen me in my social media, I am always wearing the color red. In fact, it's one of the few colors that I wear. I've had so many people ask me why I only wear red; some people get so worked up about it, but for me, it's my color.

I remember my best friend started asking me all kinds of questions as to why I only wear red. I actually wear just three colors in my wardrobe, but red is my main color. I told her why and the benefits of having minimal colors in my wardrobe.

One of the main reasons was that it helps me make decisions faster. Have you ever looked in your closet and stared at it for over an hour trying to figure out what to wear? Well that was me, and I would keep on doing this daily, especially when I used to work an office job. Then I remember reading an article about Mark Zuckerberg wearing the same outfit every day. His reason for doing that was because he wanted to use his brain power for bigger things such as running his empire and making the world a better place. I thought that made so much sense.

So I started lessening the colors in my wardrobe. I started with six colors in my wardrobe, which I eventually pared down to just three colors. I'm not as much of a stickler to the efficiency concept of Mark Zuckerberg because, I admit, I also really like buying clothes.

I also mentioned to my best friend that made it shopping and saving money easier for me since I only look for clothes in my color scheme. She asked me, "What if you found a dress you really like but they only had it green?"

I simply told her that I wouldn't buy the dress because it wasn't my color. I know that may sound a bit strange, and I'm okay with that. This is what works for me, and I love that I've been able to have a wardrobe that fits me. I'm always looking for clothes in red, and you would be surprised how difficult it can get at times to find them.

To me, wearing red signifies the color of confidence and courage and that's the energy I want to put out into the world. When there are days when I am not so confident, I wear something red to bring my confidence up and it helps me a lot. My posture and my voice are more confident when I wear my color.

Plus, everyone knows me by this color. When I walk into a room, people will notice how vibrant my red dress is or how much they like my red glasses. It's part of who I am and I love it; I won't apologize for it because it's my choice to wear this color.

Also in Chinese culture, red is considered a happy color, and you normally wear red to celebrate a birthday. My aunties would always tease me asking if it's my birthday because I constantly wear red, and I always tell them, "It's my birthday every day."

Of course they start to laugh because they think I'm funny. I also like receiving money from my relatives in a fancy red envelope called "Ang Pow" or lucky red envelope. We normally receive them when it's a special occasion such as a birthday, a wedding, or when it's Chinese New Year. So I've always associated red with good luck and wealth.

I also chose red because it is part of my culture and what it signifies. As I mentioned before, I do follow traditions that make sense, and red brings good luck, especially when it comes in a nice lucky red envelope.

Of course, everyone is different, and each color may have a different meaning for you. Choose a color that represents you or you can choose many colors that represent you. Always do what works for you; this is just what I do to build my confidence that is working for me.

The Art of Asking Questions

Never be afraid to ask questions, because if you never ask, the answer is always no.

I am big on asking questions. I don't care if the question may sound stupid to others. I want to know the answer, so I will ask away. Asking questions is what has helped me build my confidence up because it's the greatest feeling when someone says yes.

Like when I first started reaching out to women to be guests on my podcast. I have probably asked more than 1,000 women to be guest on my podcast. Have some of them said no or ghosted my emails? Of course! Have I been able to get some amazing women on my show to share their story? Yes, I have. And if I didn't go out there and simply asked these women to be on my podcast, I wouldn't have been able to interview more than 700 Asian women to date on my podcast.

Another story that I want to share is during the time that I used to work an office job. I was getting a salary review from my boss, and he gave me a raise. So my salary went from $50,000 to $54,000 that year. I asked my boss if he could increase my salary to $55,000 because in Chinese culture, anything that ends in number 4 is considered bad luck or a bad omen.

If you say the number 4 in Chinese, it also sounds like saying the word death in Chinese so you avoid that number like the plague. If you ever go to a Chinese family's house, there is no number 4 in their house number. Also, if you live in a condo building that is built by a Chinese builder, there are no floors that end in number four when you enter the elevator.

My boss laughed at me because it was the first time he'd ever heard of that belief. It didn't matter that he laughed at my Chinese beliefs; all that mattered was that he did up my salary to $55,000 that year because he respected my beliefs.

I know this may not seem like a lot. You're probably thinking, $1,000 is not a big deal. Yes, a $1,000 increase isn't a lot, but the fact that I asked for it made me realize what else could I get a yes to if I simply asked.

Woman, are often too afraid to ask for a raise because we feel like we are not good enough or we are afraid that we may get rejected for it. Of course, being rejected for that raise or that promotion is a possibility, but what if you do get that raise or get that promotion? Wouldn't that be amazing? Wouldn't that increase your confidence to another level?

Asking questions is a great way to build confidence. It's like when a guy goes out and asks a girl out for a date. He'll get rejected from hundreds of women, but once he gets a yes from one girl, he feels like he's on top of the world.

And remember even if you get a "no" when you ask your question, it's better you get a firm answer instead of you constantly wondering what if.

Learning from the "Nos"

Here's one thing you should know. You will hear no more than yes in your life. Getting rejected can bring down your confidence, but if you learn to get over it, you can move faster in your journey, and it will build up your confidence.

Plus you have to look at rejection from a different perspective. No doesn't mean no forever. Here are some ways you can look at when you get rejected:

- No could mean not right now.
- No could mean it's not the right time.
- No could mean something better is coming along.

Getting rejected definitely isn't fun. There were times where I would eat my feelings every time I got rejected (and there were *a lot* of rejections!). It helps to remember that it's not the end of the world, and you can always move past it.

Even some of the most famous people you see in the media have been rejected more times than you can imagine before they got to a "yes."

Squid Game's director Hwang Dong-hyuk was rejected by every studio he approached for 10 years before finally getting a Netflix deal. The series went on to be a viral global sensation, sweeping awards at the Golden Globes and the Emmys.

It's difficult to imagine not giving up on a dream after 10 long years. But his experience is a perfect example of how rejections don't necessarily mean that you need to stop going after your dreams. Like Hwang Dong-hyuk, getting rejected could serve as a way to learn or to discover opportunities that you never would have noticed before.

Keep Moving Forward

No matter how much you plan or prepare, life never takes a linear path. It will throw you curveballs, roadblocks, and setbacks. There are days when you will struggle or get stuck in a rut. Life can be tough but remember that there's always a way through. Everything is "figure-outable."

Being able to move forward will constantly help you build your confidence. If you fall seven times, get back up just one time more than that. You're stronger than your setbacks and roadblocks. You can conquer anything you choose, especially if you are in leadership.

A common theme in every success story is the struggle. When you look at the wins of others, you forget that it didn't come easily, and almost always took a lot of stops and starts. And the difference was, however many times they were stopped by challenges, they always got back up and started again.

A great story I want to share with you is Jo Koy's story. As a well-known comedian, easily 10,000 people would attend his comedy shows. But that's not how Jo Koy started.

In fact, he actually had a rough start. He shares his story on talk shows and on his latest Netflix special about how Netflix never wanted to buy his first comedy special. Did that stop Jo Koy from his dream? Nope. In fact, he decided to spend money to tape his own comedy special even when he was broke. When Netflix heard that Jo Koy was filming his own special, they told him not to bother with the time, money, and effort. Jo Koy went ahead and taped his own special anyway because he believed in himself, and he wasn't going to let the rejection and his current circumstances at the time get in the way of his future.

Jo Koy still went ahead and taped his special, and Netflix ended up buying it. Since then, the following has happened:

- Jo Koy has had four specials on Netflix.
- Steven Spielberg watched one of Jo Koy's comedy specials on Netflix and decided to create a movie with Jo Koy. Called *Easter Sunday*, it became the first feature film in Hollywood that showcased a Filipino family. This is history in the making.
- He is constantly selling out stadiums worldwide with his comedy tours.

One thing Jo Koy always says is that when someone tells you no, give them a reason to say yes. His story always inspires me to keep moving forward and to know that you can make things happen if you keep moving forward.

And Jo Koy wouldn't have pursued his career in comedy if it wasn't for Filipino American actress, Tia Carrere. Jo Koy mentioned in his interviews that seeing Tia Carrere on TV was the first time he thought he could be an actor or comedian in Hollywood. Back in the day, there was only a handful of Asian actors and actresses in Hollywood.

Tia Carrere shares her story about meeting Jo Koy for the first time not as a comedian but working behind the front desk in a motel in Las Vegas. When Jo Koy met Tia, he mentioned to her that his mom wanted him to be a nurse (which is a typical profession to pursue if you're Filipino), which was why he was working at the motel. In his heart, he really wanted to pursue comedy.

When Tia learned what Jo Koy really wanted to do, she advised him to just go for it. She told Jo Koy: "*Hey, man, if you can't imagine yourself doing anything else, you have to try. You have to give it a shot because I don't want you having this regret for the rest of your life. So just try and see.*"[2]

He followed that advice and is now one of the most successful comedians in the world and as his gratitude to Tia, she is also part of the cast of *Easter Sunday*.

I know it may not be easy at times or in fact all the time. I have had my fair share of setbacks, roadblocks, and times when I was in a rut. I have had many failed business attempts, failed my driving test twice, got a D in marketing in college, and, remember, I failed kindergarten for coloring outside the lines.

That never stopped me from moving forward even if I was moving at a slow pace. As long as I was taking one step forward toward my dreams and goals, that's all that mattered, and you will get there as well.

Don't Wait for the Perfect Moment

Being perfect will get you nowhere. In fact, waiting for everything to be perfect will delay your journey. You are constantly waiting for the right moment to start your business or your journey, and the truth is, there is never a right moment. You just have to start and starting messy is okay.

It can be difficult for you to start messy, especially when you grow up in a culture where you are constantly told to be perfect in everything you do. It takes a lot of unlearning on your part, but it's necessary to move forward.

I was that person: always waiting for the perfect moment to start my business. I would give myself excuses as to why I had to delay starting. I kept on delaying it to the point where 5 years passed by and I was still in the same situation, still waiting for that perfect moment to start. Had I learned to just start messy and course-correct along the way, I would have been able to achieve so much by then, but it's okay; as I said before, everything happens for a reason.

So if you are that same person who is still waiting for that perfect moment to start, do the opposite. Just start. Instead of *ready, aim, fire*, you have to *ready, fire, aim*. Keep shooting until you get it right. That's how you build confidence in yourself and in your abilities.

Be okay making mistakes and know that when you start your journey, it will not be rainbows and butterflies. When you start something new, it will be uncomfortable, awkward, and not pretty. Do it anyway because the more you keep on taking action and course-correcting along the way, the more results you will get.

My podcast is a great example of not being perfect, and I am totally okay with that. I want you to realize that even though

I have interviewed more than 700 women and have over 1.2 million downloads, it's still not perfect. Sometimes, the audio gets cut off because of the internet connection during the recording; you may also hear background noises such as monkeys in Bali or dogs barking. Even though these mistakes occur from time to time, I still can get people listening and loving the podcast. If I decided to nitpick every single mistake I made on the podcast, then there would be no podcast.

Let Go of What Others Think of You

When it comes to leadership, you have to learn to have thick skin in this game, and that means learning to let go of what others think of you. It's easier said than done, but if you let the haters affect your actions, it will delay you in your journey.

One thing you should remember is that you can't please everyone, and that's okay. If you have haters, it's a good thing because it means you are out there taking action. There were so many times I have been called racist because I empower my own community. If I let comments like that get to me, I wouldn't be here today.

A wise man once told me that you have to think about the haters as ants. They're so small that it's not going to matter when you are living life on your own terms, empowering women and becoming the leader that you are meant to be. I still remind myself of this analogy when I start to worry about what others think of me. Yes, self-doubt still creeps up on me because I'm human, but I now have the tools and support system to overcome it and move on.

When you can learn how to let go of what others think of you, it's like a heavy weight lifted off your shoulders. You are not trapped by the opinions of others. You are free to show up as your true self and become the person that you were meant to be.

Celebrate Every Win

I think we take for granted everything we have achieved in life and never celebrate it, but it's important to celebrate every win you have no matter how big or small that win may be. The more you celebrate your wins, the more confidence you will have in yourself.

During the pandemic lockdown, I had no idea how to put up a virtual background on my Zoom. I didn't realize that because I had an older laptop at the time, I had to buy a green screen to enable the virtual background. I bought the green screen, and when I was trying to figure out how the green screen feature worked, the virtual background landed on me instead of the actual background. I was about to cry until I was able to finally make it work; I was celebrating it like I just won the lottery. This may seem like such a small thing, but for me it was a win. I was able to figure it out and make it work—I felt like I could conquer anything.

It's important to celebrate every win. It gives you the feeling of what else can you conquer? What else can you achieve? You get excited and ready to move onto the next task or move forward.

I remember having a guest on my podcast who just started her business. Before we recorded the interview, I was congratulating her for leaving her job and starting her own business. My guest at the time said she will celebrate once her business becomes a success. I remember telling her that she is already a success for going out to start her own business because most people wouldn't have the guts to leave their job to start their own thing and this is a moment that needed to be celebrated. She didn't see it in that way and was happy that I mentioned that.

I always make time to celebrate every win that I have, whether it's making a $25 sale or a $1,000 sale. Never wait for the perfect moment to celebrate your wins; keep celebrating as you keep moving forward, and it will build up your confidence along the way.

Practice Makes Progress

If you want to be good at something, it will require 10,000 hours of your time. When doing anything for the first time, you'll definitely suck at it. It's important to embrace "the suck" in the beginning. Be okay with it and keep on going.

It's funny when people ask me how I got good at hosting and doing interviews. I tell them it's from being able to interview more than 700 women on my podcast that helped me get there. If you listened to my first podcast interview, I was probably a total wreck and wasn't the best. Every time I would interview another person, I would get better and better until I get people telling me how good I am. That's a result of constantly practicing my craft so that when a company hires me for a speaking gig or a hosting or interview gig, I am confident enough to give the best performance.

Another time I was confident in my ability was when I had to memorize a 10-minute speech for my group coaching session for public speaking. I was a nervous wreck at first because I was so afraid I was going to screw it up. I knew that if I wanted to give the best 10-minute speech and memorize my content, I had to practice. For about a week straight I would practice in front of the mirror at least two or three times a day so that when the actual day came, my nerves were gone, and I was able to present the content with confidence and without making so many mistakes.

My coach did enjoy the presentation and loved the content that I presented. I was able to present it within 10-minute mark that I was given. Being able to achieve this gave me the confidence that I could be a great public speaker and that wouldn't have happened if I didn't practice my speech.

When you see actors or singers on TV or live concerts, they are always constantly practicing their lines, their songs, and their dance moves to give out their best performances. It's what makes them a star. They know that they have to put in their 10,000 hours to master their craft.

If you ever see YouTube videos of K-Pop stars, they have to go through K-pop school and practice for years before they can go on stage and perform in front of an audience. So if you really want to be good at something, put in the work. Practice makes progress, which will increase your confidence.

Make the First Move

One the biggest reasons why I have been able to come so far was being a go-getter and being okay with making the first move. If I didn't make the first move with 90% of the work I have done, I wouldn't be here today. As a woman, it can be scary to go out there and make the first move, but once you start, it just takes practice, and you'll eventually get better.

As a woman, in general, you tend to wait for things to happen and because of that nothing ever happens. You keep on waiting and waiting, thinking something magical in your life will happen when you're at a standstill. You get mad and frustrated wondering why nothing is happening. That was me. I was waiting for my moment to come to me and because of that I delayed my own success for 5 years. When I decided to start making moves and reaching out to people, that's when I started getting the things that I wanted.

As a woman, you have always been brought up that way. It's like dating. You wait for a guy to ask you out on a date because it would be wrong and desperate of you to make the first move and ask a guy out or ask for his number. People will start talking about how awful it was for you to make the first move with a guy you like, and because of that, you don't make the first move. You end up waiting, hoping, and wishing he's going to ask you out.

Isn't it insane how much women get judged if they do something that is not typical? It's worse when other women judge you for it, and you wonder why women in general aren't advancing as much as men.

Hollywood and Disney doesn't help in improving this mindset at all. How many storylines do you see where a woman is waiting for "Prince Charming" to come and save her from her awful situation? Cinderella is one of my all-time favorite movies as a child, and when I mean favorite, I mean I watched it religiously, every day to the point where I started singing the theme song in front of everyone at my aunt's wedding ceremony when I was her flower girl.

But when you really think about the story, Cinderella is in a terrible situation in which she is treated poorly by her stepmother and stepsisters. To get out of that situation, her Prince Charming swoops her away her from her misery, they get married, and live happily ever after. I don't believe that getting married just days after meeting someone leads to "happily ever after," the reality is marriage takes a lot of work from both sides of the relationship. The trouble is, we grew up with this thinking that having a good life and a happy ending depends on finding a man and getting married.

And then you constantly obsess about this because it's all you ever see in movies and TV shows. You keep waiting for the Prince Charming to save you when the only person who can really save you is you. I'm not saying that being with someone is bad; I think you have to be with someone for the right reasons. You want to be with someone because that person is your person who will be there for you through good and bad times and will love you unconditionally flaws and all. The fairytale that Hollywood paints can give a distorted perception of how things are supposed to work for women.

So, if you want to become a leader, there is no waiting game. If you want things to change for yourself, you have to make the first move, even if it's scary. It wasn't a walk in the park for me as well. It was difficult at first to reach out to different people but with time, it got easier, and the more I made the first move, the more opportunities came my way. And because more opportunities came my way, my confidence level grew.

If reaching out to people is challenging for you, just remember that there are three outcomes you will have. They'll say yes, they'll say no, or they'll ghost you. If you're okay with these outcomes, then you move forward. You won't die; you just move onto the next person.

I see very few Asian women who will go out there and make things happen or become a go-getter. When I attend networking events, very few Asian women go, which is disappointing for me. I even had a conversation about this with a fellow Asian woman who is a leader in the community, and she mentioned the same thing. As an Asian woman, you have to learn to reach out, make the first move, and become a go-getter if you want to become a leader.

Ask for Help

While being a go-getter is a big factor in building confidence, having the courage to ask for help was another big factor in my confidence boost. It was hard for me in the beginning to reach out and ask for a referral or support, but the more I kept doing this, the easier it got for me, and I was able to move forward faster.

What most people don't realize is that I am a very stubborn person. Sometimes it can work for me, and other times it can work against me. In this situation, my stubbornness worked against me since I was too proud to ask for help, and because I never asked for help, I stunted my own growth in building confidence and becoming the leader that I was meant to be.

It is very important to remind yourself that it's totally okay for you to ask for help. You don't have to be in this journey by yourself. You are reading this book for a reason; you want to learn what it means to be a leader and how to go about it.

I can understand that it can be difficult to ask for help, especially if you grew up in a culture like mine where you are told that asking for help is considered as a sign of weakness or you are asking for a handout. Both of those reasons are totally untrue. Being able to ask for help is what made me build my confidence a lot faster because there's someone cheering me on and has my back no matter what I am going through. Being able to have a support system is what I needed the most, especially in this journey of forging my own path.

There is no shame in asking for help especially if you want to accelerate building your confidence and become a leader. It's also better when you do things together. Now is not the time to think it's uncool to ask for help.

There are so many ways for you to ask for help as well. You can hire a coach, have an accountability partner, read books, join a women's group, listen to podcasts, and more. I am truly grateful for my support system. I can reach out to them anytime through the good and bad times. If I am in a rut, my support system will be there to cheer me up and remind me of my greatness.

What most people don't realize is that you have so many blind spots that can delay your success. Asking for help is crucial and can help you move forward more quickly than if you tried to figure it out alone.

It's like driving a car. You have rearview mirrors to reduce the blind spots when you are driving. Without your mirrors, how can you feel safe to get to where you are going or keep you from hitting anyone or anything?

Confidence plays a big part in leadership, and you can see how far you can go when your confidence increases. I can't believe we are getting to the last chapter where I start sharing about the future of Asian women leadership. I'm sure you are curious as to what that may look like, so let's turn the page to the next and last chapter of this book.

8

The Future of Asian Women in Leadership

In recent years, Asian women have made many strides when it comes to leadership and opening doors for all women. There have been some great Asian women out there who have made history for us. Here are some notable Asian women who have made the impossible possible.

Kamala Harris

Kamala Harris is the first woman to be elected vice president of the United States. She holds the highest ranking female official in US history along with being the first African American and Asian American woman vice president. While Kamala Harris was sworn in as vice president, parents sent in photos of little girls watching and made a video montage of it. Being able to see the little girls watch Kamala sworn in as vice president is giving them hope that one day they can also have the highest seat in the White House and beyond.[1]

Kim Ng

You may not have heard of Kim Ng before, but she's a woman who has made history in the sports world. Kim Ng is the first woman to be hired as a general manager in any major sports team and the first East Asian American to lead a Major League Baseball team. In November 2020, she became the general manager for the Miami Marlins. Kim has had her fair share of challenges to get to where she is today. While her track record has been amazing, she was rejected at least 10 times as general manager for previous teams.[2]

If you talk to any baseball fan, they will tell you that Kim has a great track record when it comes to winning the World Series. She is no joke; in fact, a lot of men were celebrating her success for becoming a general manager because, according to them, it's about damn time! If a guy had her track record, he would have instantly gotten the general manager position without any hesitation but because Kim was an Asian woman, there was more pushback.

I am so glad that Kim Ng never gave up and kept moving forward. Because of her efforts, she opened doors for so many women to have a high position in a major sports team.

Wave (Marvel Superhero)

While this is a fictional character, to me it is still a very monumental moment for Asian women. On International Women's Day 2019, Marvel introduced the Filipina superhero named Wave.[3] This one hits a little closer to home because Wave grew up and lives in Cebu City where I was born.

Another thing that I like about Wave is her physical features. She has morena skin, which means she has a darker brown complexion. This is so important since the beauty standards in the Philippines always favors pearly white skin and having a darker skin complexion is considered not as beautiful.

Being able to create this character can show littles girls that Asian women can be superheroes as well. I hope by the time you read this, Wave has already made an appearance in a Marvel show or movie.

Janet Yang

Janet Yang has been a voice for Asian representation in Hollywood for decades. In 2022, she became the first Asian American to be named as the new president of the Academy of Motion Picture Arts and Sciences. Janet has work with big name directors like Steven Spielberg and previously worked on famous movies such as *The Joy Luck Club* and *The People vs. Larry Flynt*.[4]

Janet Yang is truly a person who has opened doors for so many Asian Americans to break into Hollywood. She is also known as "the godmother of Asian Americans in Hollywood." If you are ever in Los Angeles and happen to stop by the Academy Museum of Motion Pictures, a pillar was dedicated and named in her honor.[5]

Sandra Oh

Sandra Oh is one my favorite actresses and my big role model, especially since, like me, she's also from Canada. Sandra Oh has been able to make a name for herself and be able to break barriers when it comes to Asian representation in Hollywood. Some of her achievements include being the first person of Asian descent to host the Golden Globes. She's also the first Asian actress in 39 years to win a Golden Globe for Best Actress in a TV series and the first Asian actress to win more than one Golden Globe.[6]

Aside from breaking barriers and making waves in Hollywood, she's always advocating for the Asian American community and people of color. She uses her influence and visibility as she joins protests, walking side by side with the community, and speaking up and calling out the injustices the Asian community faces. I love that she is so proud of her Asian heritage. In her own words: "*It's an honor just to be Asian.*"

BLACKPINK

The biggest girl group in the world hails from South Korea by the name of BLACKPINK. The K-pop girl group consists of four women by the names of Lisa, Jennie, Jisoo, and Rosé. BLACKPINK has been able to grace the covers of big-time magazines such as *Rolling Stone*, headline concerts such as Coachella, and rack up billions of views on their music videos. They also have the most YouTube subscribers for any musical act in YouTube history, dethroning Justin Bieber.[7]

This is a huge accomplishment because for so long, North America never took foreign artists seriously, especially if they didn't sing in English. Radio stations refused to play non-English songs.

While BLACKPINK does have some songs in English, most of their songs are in Korean, and they still have been able to create worldwide domination with their hit songs. BLACKPINK literally has fans from all over the world, and their fans are called Blinks. They have been able to collaborate with big-name artists in the United States such as Selena Gomez.

BLACKPINK is paving the way for so many Asian artists out there. I just love that they have been able to break records time and time again. They have shown the world that Asian women can be bankable worldwide. You can see them represent big brand names like Chanel, and they even have big billboards in New York City.

Savitri Jindal

You may not have heard of Savitri Jindal, but she is currently the richest Asian woman in the world with an estimated net worth of $18 billion. Even though Savitri inherited her fortune from her late husband, she was able to triple her net worth from $4.8 billion to $17.7 billion after she took charge of the company.[8]

Not only is Savitri the richest Asian woman in the world, she is also one of the top 10 wealthiest individuals in India.

I love her story because women are rarely taken seriously when they are in CEO positions, but Savitri was able to prove to everyone that not only could she run the company, but she also took the company to a whole new level. Her current net worth is proof that she is a leader in the business world.

Rosa Saito

This woman is definitely a leader in her own right. Rosa Saito decided to pursue a modeling career at the age of 68 and took the fashion industry by storm. At 71, she continues to have a successful career modeling and breaks all kinds of barriers for women. This is huge since you always think it's too late to start something new, especially if you are a woman who is older. You can literally start at any given moment, and Rosa is a great example of that.

Rosa is inspiring everyone to go after their dreams and not let age get in the way of your circumstances.

I could mention many more Asian women leaders who have been able to pave the way for us, but it would end up being such a long chapter, which is a good problem to have. If you check out my podcast, The Tao of Self-Confidence, there are interviews with more than 700 Asian women who share their inner journey to self-confidence that you can definitely relate to.

I truly believe that Asian women are a force to be reckoned with. I have met so many amazing Asian women who have been able to show you what is possible. More Asian women are speaking up and calling out the injustices that you see. I have witnessed Asian women who understand their worth and have learned to walk away from things that don't serve them.

While the numbers are still low, we are taking the right steps to be seen as leaders, and the more steps we take, the more we will be seen and heard by the world. I also believe that our efforts will also affect the world, as seen by the previous examples of the phenomenal Asian women who have broken barriers for all women.

The future looks bright as the younger generation is seeing more representation in all industries, whether it's politics or entertainment. I never had that kind of representation at all growing up, which made it difficult for me to see myself as someone worthy to take up space in this world. Now I see little girls who want to become president one day or become a singer because they see someone who looks like them open the doors to new opportunities and break the glass ceilings they have faced for years.

It's great to see the younger generation create advocacy groups to fight injustices such as racism in North America. Because they see someone fighting for them, they can join forces to create a positive impact in the world. In the end, you have the power to create the change you wish to see in this world.

There's no better time than now to support more women leaders. Let's keep on moving forward even if life make us go one step forward and two steps back. A recent report from McKinsey mentioned that Asian American women in corporate leadership roles dropped 80%.[9]

The report may make it seem that we're not moving forward, but don't let that data discourage you. There will always be challenges, no matter what happens in your journey, and you must learn how to push through those hard times. If you read the stories about other leaders, they always go through some form of pushback, even with their accomplishments and success.

Encountering pushback may also be a good indicator that we're heading in the right direction. We've been in the background for so long, especially because of cultural expectations and upbringing, that sometimes we need to carve our own path.

Now that we've built this momentum, we have to keep moving forward if we want to develop leaders.

Conclusion: Words for Your Self-Confidence Journey

As someone who has felt (and classified by the world as) invisible, it was so hard to see myself as anything more than what was expected of me. I followed the path that was set out for me by my parents, my relatives, and my culture because that was all I knew. It was really hard for me to imagine anything outside of that path because there was nobody I could look up to who paved the way.

I ended up always following the crowd, looking for constant approval, and I lost my true sense of self in the process. I was truly afraid to decide for myself and live the way I wanted because my experiences taught me not to trust others and my own self. It was hard for me to trust my instincts and make any moves because I always feared the unknown instead of looking at it as an opportunity. I took life for granted and never really "lived" because I strived for safety and stability, which left me feeling stuck and resentful of myself.

It took the death of a close family member for me to realize that life is so precious and can be gone in an instant. I knew if I kept going the safe path, I wasn't really living. That moment made me realize I had to give myself permission to start living for myself instead of fulfilling the expectations of others. In my journey, things were definitely messy, but it was my beautiful hot mess that led me to where I am today.

Never in a million years did I think I would be writing a book talking about confidence and leadership for women. If you asked me 15 years ago what my life was going to be like now, I would probably tell you that I would still be working an office job until I retire because that was the definition of success that was laid out for me; I believed it for so long.

The more I realize I was able to do more than what was set out for me, I was able to go on this messy journey to building confidence in myself and for my community. It all led to this book. If my younger self saw this today, she would have given me the biggest hug ever for writing a book that not only talks about leadership but also gives a voice to a community that is still invisible to this day.

I hope this book leads you to the same messy, wonderful journey to self-confidence as my experiences have done for me. This book went deep into the Asian cultural and historical background because it plays a big part in figuring out what has stopped women, especially Asian women, from advancing into leadership roles.

And while this book does focus on Asian culture, it's still a book that women from all walks of life can relate to or see things from a different perspective. We share similar issues as women, no matter our differences in heritage.

I hope this book helps you reflect on what you've gone through in your life and shows you ways to heal so that you can show up stronger than ever. Your journey is something that you'll be working on daily as new things come up: new roadblocks, new challenges, and new setbacks. Don't let that stop you; instead let it fuel you to keep moving forward.

The most important thing you can do after reading this book is to take action. Knowledge is great, but it's useless if you don't apply it to your daily life.

Taking action can be scary, especially if this is all new for you. My advice for someone who is very new on their journey is to just take it one step at a time. You don't have to make big leaps to create big changes. In fact, the biggest changes are made by small, actionable daily steps. It's okay to make mistakes and course-correct along the way. Your journey will always be a process and will never be perfect.

I encourage you to read this book as many times as you need. Sometimes reading it for the first time, you won't be able to catch everything. Some of the things I wrote here may make more sense to you when you read it the second or third time. You could also take notes or highlight parts of the book that resonate with you the most. This is your journey, and you choose what works for you.

Know that you are more capable than you realize. It's how you perceive yourself that's stopping you from your greatness. I believe that women face a huge confidence gap from men, partly because of mindset. Men aren't innately smarter than women; they're just willing to take action regardless of the outcome. If women did the same thing, imagine how much we can achieve.

Last, I want to remind you that it's okay to seek and ask for help. I know I've mentioned this several times throughout the book. You don't have to be alone in this journey. Have the confidence and courage to ask for help. Your future self will thank you for it.

I hope that I'll get a chance to meet you one day and hear your stories of how you went from trauma to triumph. One of the things I love the most is hearing an underdog story. You can literally change your circumstances at any given moment, and the only person you need permission from to forge your own path is yourself.

Keep moving forward! You've got this, queen!

Notes

Chapter 1

1. Caliendo, S.M. and McIlwain, C.D. (2020). *The Routledge companion to race and ethnicity*. [online]. Google Books. Routledge, pp. 173–176. Available from: https://books.google.com.ph/books?id=Iqf7DwAAQBAJ&source=gbs_navlinks_s [Accessed 9 Dec. 2022].
2. Pettersen, W. (2010). *Success story, Japanese-American style* [online]. Available from: http://inside.sfuhs.org/dept/history/US_History_reader/Chapter14/modelminority.pdf.
3. encyclopedia.densho.org. (n.d.). *Model minority* [online]. Available from: https://encyclopedia.densho.org/Model_minority.
4. *US News & World Report*. (1966). Success story of one minority group in US [online]. *US News and World Report*, 26 Dec., pp. 6–9. Available from: https://www.dartmouth.edu/~hist32/Hist33/US%20News%20&%20World%20Report.pdf.
5. Song, C. (2019). *10 facts to help you understand Chinese culture* [online]. China Highlights. Available from: https://www.chinahighlights.com/travelguide/chinese-culture-facts.htm.
6. Reja, M. (2021). *Trump's 'Chinese Virus' tweet helped lead to rise in racist anti-Asian Twitter content: Study* [online]. ABC News. Available from: https://abcnews.go.com/Health/trumps-chinese-virus-tweet-helped-lead-rise-racist/story?id=76530148.

7. Lapin, T. (2021). Grandmother brutally beaten on LA bus by attacker who thought she was Asian. *New York Post* [online]. Available from: https://nypost.com/2021/04/16/grandmother-brutally-beaten-on-la-bus-by-attacker-who-thought-she-was-asian.
8. Kids-world-travel-guide.com. (2018). *Asia facts for kids* [online]. Available from: https://www.kids-world-travel-guide.com/asia-facts.html.
9. Xiao, B. (2021). *A closer look: Behind the rise in anti-Asian attacks* [online]. Epoch Times. Available from: https://www.theepochtimes.com/a-closer-look-behind-the-rise-in-anti-asian-hate_3739723.html.
10. Wong, B. (2022). *7 ways the "model minority" myth hurts Asian American's mental health* [online]. HuffPost. Available from: https://www.huffpost.com/entry/model-minority-myth-asian-american-mental-health_l_628d470de4b0b1d9844e3297.

Chapter 2

1. Kornfield, M. and Knowles, H. (2021). Captain who said spa shootings suspect had 'bad day' no longer a spokesman on case, official says. *Washington Post* [online]. 18 Mar. Available from: https://www.washingtonpost.com/nation/2021/03/17/jay-baker-bad-day.
2. Hoang, K.K. (2021). *How the history of spas and sex work fits into the conversation about the Atlanta shootings* [online]. Vox. Available from: https://www.vox.com/first-person/22338462/atlanta-shooting-georgia-spa-asian-american.
3. UCA News. (n.d.). *The Philippines' secret pandemic of child sexual abuse* [online]. Available from: https://www.ucanews.com/news/the-philippines-secret-pandemic-of-child-sexual-abuse/96695.
4. McGeough, S. (2022). *Human trafficking in the Philippines* [online]. The Exodus Road. Available from: https://theexodusroad.com/human-trafficking-in-the-philippines.
5. thediplomat.com. (n.d.). *ASEAN urged to intervene over human trafficking* [online]. Available from: https://thediplomat.com/2022/09/asean-urged-to-intervene-over-human-trafficking.
6. BGSU Libraries. (2019). *Asian immigration: The "Yellow Peril." Race in the United States, 1880–1940.* [online]. Available from: https://digitalgallery.bgsu.edu/student/exhibits/show/race-in-us/asian-americans/asian-immigration-and-the--yel.
7. BGSU Libraries. (2019). *Asian immigration: The "Yellow Peril." Race in the United States, 1880–1940.* [online]. Available from: https://

digitalgallery.bgsu.edu/student/exhibits/show/race-in-us/asian-americans/asian-immigration-and-the--yel

8. Rodriguez, M. (2016). *NBC's upcoming "Mail Order Family" is about a man who orders a Filipina mail-order bride* [online]. MIC. Available from: https://www.mic.com/articles/155495/nbc-s-upcoming-mail-order-family-is-about-a-man-who-orders-a-filipina-mail-order-bride.
9. Gao, M. (2022). It's Michelle Yeoh's universe. We're All just living in it. *ELLE* [online]. Available from: https://www.elle.com/culture/movies-tv/a39763674/michelle-yeoh-everything-everywhere-all-at-once-interview.
10. LinkedIn. (n.d.a). *Sheena Yap Chan on LinkedIn: #stopasianhate* [online]. Available from: https://www.linkedin.com/posts/sheenayapchan_stopasianhate-activity-6911794019924627456-y0BZ [Accessed 17 Nov. 2022].
11. LinkedIn (n.d.b). *Sheena Yap Chan on LinkedIn: Media loves putting an Asian woman on the front cover when it comes to… [online].* Available from: https://www.linkedin.com/posts/sheenayapchan_stopasianhate-endracism-activity-6928791436184186881-cMPO [Accessed 17 Nov. 2022].
12. LinkedIn. (n.d.c). *Sheena Yap Chan on LinkedIn: Every time there's a new Covid variant that comes up, media always* [online]. Available from: https://www.linkedin.com/posts/sheenayapchan_everytime-theres-a-new-covid-variant-that-activity-6955223000686206976-tAcW [Accessed 17 Nov. 2022].
13. www1.nyc.gov. (n.d.). *Stop Asian hate* [online]. Available from: https://www1.nyc.gov/site/cchr/community/stop-asian-hate.page.
14. Celona, L. and Moore, T. (2022). Asian woman, 65, attacked and robbed on tree-lined street in Queens [online]. *New York Post*. Available from: https://nypost.com/2022/07/10/asian-woman-65-attacked-and-robbed-in-nyc-neighborhood [Accessed 17 Nov. 2022].
15. Austin Chronicle. (2022). *Asian mail order brides: Your guide to Asian women for marriage* [online]. Available from: https://www.austinchronicle.com/daily/sponsored/2022-06-24/asian-mail-order-brides [Accessed 17 Nov. 2022].
16. Tamanaha, A. (2022). *Sponsored posts advertising Asian mail order brides spark outrage* [online]. AsAmNews. Available from: https://asamnews.com/2022/06/28/austin-chronicle-sf-weekly-sponsored-posts-advertising-asian-mail-order-brides-spark-outrage [Accessed 17 Nov. 2022].

17. Martinache, J. (2022). *Top Asian cam sites: The best Asian webcam models and online cams* [online]. Washington City Paper. Available from: https://washingtoncitypaper.com/article/554093/top-asian-cam-sites-the-best-asian-webcam-models-and-online-cams [Accessed 17 Nov. 2022].

18. Zweigenhaft, R.L. (2021). *Who rules America: Diversity among Fortune 500 CEOs from 2000 to 2020* [online]. https://whorulesamerica.ucsc.edu/power/diversity_update_2020.html.

19. University of Redlands. (2021). *Asian names in the workplace* [online]. Available from: https://ocpd.redlands.edu/blog/2021/05/24/asian-names-in-the-workplace.

20. Wikipedia Contributors. (2019). *Sheng nu* [online]. Wikipedia. Available from: https://en.wikipedia.org/wiki/Sheng_nu.

21. Anon. (2022). *Valentine's day in China: When the Communist Party plays matchmaker* [online]. Available from: https://gettotext.com/valentines-day-in-china-when-the-communist-party-plays-matchmaker [Accessed 17 Nov. 2022].

22. Wikipedia. (2022). *Christmas cake* [online]. Available from: https://en.wikipedia.org/wiki/Christmas_cake [Accessed 17 Nov. 2022].

23. worldpopulationreview.com. (n.d.). *Arranged marriage countries 2021 [online]*. Available from: https://worldpopulationreview.com/country-rankings/arranged-marriage-countries.

24. Editorial staff. (2022). *Chinese woman facing nonstop pressure from her parents to get married develops severe anxiety disorder* [online]. NextShark. Available from: https://nextshark.com/chinese-woman-marriage-anxiety [Accessed 17 Nov. 2022].

25. Noor-Oshiro, A. (2021). *Asian American young adults are the only racial group with suicide as their leading cause of death, so why is no one talking about this?* [online] The Conversation. Available from: https://theconversation.com/asian-american-young-adults-are-the-only-racial-group-with-suicide-as-their-leading-cause-of-death-so-why-is-no-one-talking-about-this-158030.

26. Trevor Project. (2021). *The Trevor Project National Survey* [online]. www.thetrevorproject.org. Available from: https://www.thetrevorproject.org/survey-2021/?section=Introduction.

27. Hall, R. (2021). *Women of color spend more than $8 billion on bleaching creams worldwide every year [online]*. The Conversation. Available from: https://theconversation.com/women-of-color-spend-more-than-8-billion-on-bleaching-creams-worldwide-every-year-153178.

28. Wong, L. (2021). *Asian beauty standards and its negative consequences* [online]. Work In Progress. Available from: https://www.workinprogressmag.com/post/asian-beauty-standards-and-its-negative-consequences.
29. Gasteratos, K., Spyropoulou, G.-A. and Suess, L. (2021). "Zoom dysmorphia": A new diagnosis in the COVID-19 pandemic era? *Plastic & Reconstructive Surgery*, publish ahead of print. doi:10.1097/prs.0000000000008559. Available from: https://journals.lww.com/plasreconsurg/Fulltext/2021/12000/_Zoom_Dysmorphia___A_New_Diagnosis_in_the_COVID_19.74.aspx.
30. The Confidence Code for Girls. (n.d.). *The confidence collapse and why it matters for the next gen* [online]. Available from: https://static1.squarespace.com/static/588b93f6bf629a6bec7a3bd2/t/5ac39193562fa73cd8a07a89/1522766258986/The+Confidence+Code+for+Girls+x+Ypulse.pdf.
31. Radio Free Asia. (n.d.). *Homes before husbands: Why younger Chinese women put their trust in real estate* [online]. Available from: https://www.rfa.org/english/news/china/trust-01112022094623.html [Accessed 17 Nov. 2022].
32. Unicef. (n.d.). *Ending child marriage and adolescent empowerment* [online]. Available from: https://www.unicef.org/india/what-we-do/end-child-marriage.
33. ProBono India. (n.d.). *Widowhood in India* [online]. Available from: https://www.probono-india.in/blog-detail.php?id=172 [Accessed 17 Nov. 2022].
34. World Economic Forum. (2022). *Global gender gap report*. Available from: https://www3.weforum.org/docs/WEF_GGGR_2022.pdf.
35. East Asia Forum. (2022). *Japan's stubborn gender inequality problem* [online]. Available from: https://www.eastasiaforum.org/2022/06/28/japans-stubborn-gender-inequality-problem.

Chapter 3

1. bestofkorea.com. (2022). *Breaking the cycle of intergenerational trauma in "Umma"* [online]. Available from: https://bestofkorea.com/umma-breaking-the-cycle-of-intergenerational-trauma [Accessed 17 Nov. 2022].
2. DC Coalition to End Sexual Violence. (2022). *Sexual assault awareness month 2022: Community-specific facts and statistics*. Available from: https://static1.squarespace.com/static/58c1bbf8440243d83e846273/t/6246a9f97fefa74d5b611300/1648798201678/Community-Specific+Facts+-+SAAM+2022.pdf.

3. World Health Organization. (2021). *Devastatingly pervasive: 1 in 3 women globally experience violence* [online]. https://www.who.int/news/item/09-03-2021-devastatingly-pervasive-1-in-3-women-globally-experience-violence.
4. Jiang, F. (2019). *Ancient Chinese marriage customs* [online]. China Highlights. Available from: https://www.chinahighlights.com/travelguide/culture/ancient-chinese-marriage-customs.htm.
5. Angelli. (2020). *How did women from Joseon dynasty live their lives?* [online] uBitto. https://ubitto.com/blog/culture/how-did-women-from-joseon-dynasty-live-their-lives.
6. Koushik, B. (2021). *5 old Indian customs that denied women human rights* [online]. History of Yesterday. Available from: https://medium.com/history-of-yesterday/5-old-indian-customs-that-denied-women-human-rights-64a4683c01d9 [Accessed 17 Nov. 2022].
7. Wikipedia. (2020). *Page Act of 1875* [online]. Available from: https://en.wikipedia.org/wiki/Page_Act_of_1875.
8. Kuo, K. and Leong, K. (2021). *US has a long history of violence against Asian women* [online]. The Conversation. Available from: https://theconversation.com/us-has-a-long-history-of-violence-against-asian-women-157533.
9. Kipling, R. (1929). *"The White Man's Burden": Kipling's hymn to US imperialism* [online]. Gmu.edu. Available from: http://historymatters.gmu.edu/d/5478.
10. Mitra, D., Kang, S. and Clutario, G. (2021). *It's time to reckon with the history of Asian women in America* [online]. Harper's BAZAAR. Available from: https://www.harpersbazaar.com/culture/features/a35913981/its-time-to-reckon-with-the-history-of-asian-women-in-america.
11. Blakemore, E. (2019). *The brutal history of Japan's "comfort women"* [online]. History. Available from: https://www.history.com/news/comfort-women-japan-military-brothels-korea.

Chapter 4

1. Tull, M. (2021). *What is trauma?* [online]. Verywell Mind. Available from: https://www.verywellmind.com/common-symptoms-after-a-traumatic-event-2797496.
2. Cooper, S. (2022). *Women's mental health: Facts and statistics* [online]. Available from: https://www.innerbody.com/womens-mental-health-facts-and-statistics.

3. Center for Child Trauma Assessment and Service Planning. (2015). *What is child trauma?* [online] Available from: https://cctasi.northwestern.edu/child-trauma/.
4. Associated Press. (2022). *Man punches father, child in suspected anti-Asian bias crime* [online]. U.S. News & World Report. https://www.usnews.com/news/best-states/oregon/articles/2022-07-04/man-punches-father-child-in-suspected-anti-asian-bias-crime.
5. Lee, H. and KTVU staff. (2022). *Co-owner of Filipino restaurant in Oakland shot dead in front of son* [online]. Available from: https://www.ktvu.com/news/filipino-restaurant-says-co-owner-of-lucky-three-seven-killed-in-oakland.amp [Accessed 17 Nov. 2022].
6. Center for Child Trauma Assessment and Service Planning. (2015). *What is child trauma?* [online]. Available from: https://cctasi.northwestern.edu/child-trauma/.
7. WebMD. (2003). *Posttraumatic stress disorder (PTSD)* [online]. WebMD. Availablefrom:https://www.webmd.com/mental-health/post-traumatic-stress-disorder.
8. DerSarkissian, C. (2017). *Symptoms of PTSD* [online]. WebMD. Available from: https://www.webmd.com/mental-health/what-are-symptoms-ptsd.
9. Julia, N. (2022). *Post-traumatic stress disorder (PTSD) statistics: 2022 update* [online]. CFAH. Available from: https://cfah.org/ptsd-statistics.
10. Pacific Grove Hospital. (2018). *Signs and symptoms of posttraumatic stress disorder* [online]. Pacific Grove. Available from: https://www.pacificgrovehospital.com/ptsd/symptoms-signs-effects.
11. Vantage Point Recovery (n.d.). *PTSD causes: The 4 most common causes of PTSD & treatment* [online]. Available from: https://vantagepointrecovery.com/ptsd-causes/.
12. Hull, M. (2022). *PTSD facts and statistics* [online]. The Recovery Village Drug and Alcohol Rehab. Available from: https://www.therecoveryvillage.com/mental-health/ptsd/ptsd-statistics.
13. Schermele, Z. (n.d.). *Following criticism of Asian mail-order bride ad, newsweekly halts sponsored posts* [online]. Available from: https://www.nbcnews.com/news/asian-america/criticism-asian-mail-order-bride-ad-newsweekly-halts-sponsored-posts-rcna36174 [Accessed 17 Nov. 2022].
14. National Coalition Against Domestic Violence. (2021). *Statistics* [online]. Available from: https://ncadv.org/statistics.

15. UN Women. (2020). *The shadow pandemic: Violence against women during COVID-19* [online]. Available from: https://www.unwomen.org/en/news/in-focus/in-focus-gender-equality-in-covid-19-response/violence-against-women-during-covid-19.
16. American Psychiatry Association. (n.d.). *Mental health facts for Asian Americans/Pacific Islanders* [online]. Available from: https://www.psychiatry.org/File%20Library/Psychiatrists/Cultural-Competency/Mental-Health-Disparities/Mental-Health-Facts-for-Asian-Americans-Pacific-Islanders.pdf.
17. Stop AAPI Hate. (n.d.). *Two years and thousands of voices*. Available from: https://stopaapihate.org/wp-content/uploads/2022/07/Stop-AAPI-Hate-Year-2-Report.pdf.
18. A curious public servant. (2022). *Eliminate hate: Addressing Anti-Asian racism* [online]. Government of Canada. Available from: https://www.canada.ca/en/government/system/digital-government/living-digital/ahm.html.
19. Daily Bruin. (2021). *Opinion: Poor media coverage of anti-Asian hate crimes worsens historical issues* [online]. Available from: https://dailybruin.com/2021/04/26/opinion-poor-media-coverage-of-anti-asian-hate-crimes-worsens-historical-issues.
20. Dastin, J. (2022). *Amazon makes first venture fund bets with $150 mln for underrepresented founders*. Reuters [online]. Available from: https://www.reuters.com/business/finance/amazon-makes-first-venture-fund-bets-with-150-mln-underrepresented-founders-2022-10-05.
21. CBS News. (n.d.). *Asian woman hit with racism while at concert at Irvine Amphitheater* [online]. Available from: https://www.cbsnews.com/losangeles/news/asian-woman-hit-with-racism-while-at-concert-at-irvine-amphitheater [Accessed 22 Nov. 2022].
22. Connley, C. (2021). *In 1 year, women globally lost $800 billion in income due to Covid-19, new report finds* [online]. CNBC. Available from: https://www.cnbc.com/2021/04/30/women-globally-lost-800-billion-dollars-in-income-due-to-covid-19.html.
23. Batista, J. (2017). *The Confucianism-feminism conflict: Why a new understanding is necessary* [online]. Schwarzman Scholars. Available from: https://www.schwarzmanscholars.org/events-and-news/confucianism-feminism-conflict-new-understanding-necessary.
24. Hays, J. (n.d.). *Women in Vietnam: Traditional views, advances and abuse* [online] factsanddetails.com. Available from: https://factsanddetails.com/southeast-asia/Vietnam/sub5_9c/entry-3390.html#chapter-1.

25. Park, J. (2020). *7 questions to ask yourself when you're feeling down* [online]. Asian Mental Health Collective. Available from: https://www.asianmhc.org/7-questions-to-ask-yourself-when-youre-feeling-down [Accessed 22 Nov. 2022].

Chapter 5

1. Tu, J. (2022). *No girls remain in Hawaii's Youth Correctional Facility* [online]. Women's Agenda. Available from: https://womensagenda.com.au/latest/no-girls-remain-in-hawaiis-youth-correctional-facility [Accessed 22 Nov. 2022].
2. Allard, S. (2021). *Sanskrit words you might be pronouncing incorrectly* [online]. Hindu American Foundation. Available from: https://www.hinduamerican.org/blog/sanskrit-words-pronouncing-incorrectly [Accessed 22 Nov. 2022].
3. Hands on Health. (2020). *The seven chakras and their meanings* [online]. Hands on Health Sheffield. Available from: http://www.handsonhealthsheffield.com/holistic_massage/the-seven-chakras-for-beginners.
4. Bontempo, K. (n.d.). *Asian-American women and mental health care* [online]. www.ourtownny.com. Available from: https://www.ourtownny.com/news/asian-american-women-and-mental-health-care-CH2081422 [Accessed 22 Nov. 2022].
5. Chang, J. (2022). *A deep dive into your favorite K-dramas from a mental health perspective*. Noonas Noonchi [online]. Available from: https://noonasnoonchi.com [Accessed 28 Nov. 2022].

Chapter 6

1. Deloitte. (2022). *Women @ Work 2022: A global outlook* [online]. Available from: https://www2.deloitte.com/content/dam/Deloitte/global/Documents/deloitte-women-at-work-2022-a-global-outlook.pdf.
2. Georgia HOPE. (n.d.). July: Self-care month – Georgia HOPE [online]. Available from: https://gahope.org/july-self-care-month [Accessed 22 Nov. 2022].
3. Blurt Foundation. (2020). *Self-care vs. self-love: What's the difference?* [online] Available from: https://www.blurtitout.org/2020/09/24/self-care-vs-self-love-whats-difference.

4. Body Shop. (n.d.) Self-love Global Index [online]. Available from: https://thebodyshop.a.bigcontent.io/v1/static/019-Q1-2021-selflove-self-love-index-pdf-3.

Chapter 7

1. Peterson, T.J. (n.d.). *What is self-confidence?*. HealthyPlace. [online] Availablefrom:https://www.healthyplace.com/self-help/self-confidence/what-is-self-confidence.
2. Ragusa, G. (2022). *Jo Koy's sweet connection to "Easter Sunday" star Tia Carrere—How she inspired him when he was a hotel front desk clerk [Exclusive]* [online]. Showbiz Cheat Sheet. Available from: https://www.cheatsheet.com/entertainment/tia-carrere-reveals-sweet-connection-easter-sunday-comedian-jo-koy-front-desk-clerk.html [Accessed 22 Nov. 2022].

Chapter 8

1. ABC7 San Francisco. (2021). *"Truly indescribable": Girls around US watch with awe, admiration as Kamala Harris is sworn in as vice president* [online]. Available from: https://abc7news.com/kamala-harris-first-female-vice-president-glass-ceiling-inauguration/9879256 [Accessed 22 Nov. 2022].
2. Gregory, S. (2021). *How Kim Ng, MLB's first female GM, finally got the top job* [online]. Time. Available from: https://time.com/5943601/kim-ng-first-female-gm-miami-marlins.
3. Sugbo.ph (2019). *Marvel's new Filipina superhero is a Cebuana!* [online]. Sugbo.ph. Available from: https://sugbo.ph/2019/first-filipino-marvel-superhero [Accessed 22 Nov. 2022].
4. Davis, C. (2022). *Janet Yang becomes first Asian elected as Film Academy president* [online]. Variety. Available from: https://variety.com/2022/awards/news/janet-yang-president-film-academy-1235331853/amp [Accessed 22 Nov. 2022].
5. Feinberg, S. (2022). *Janet Yang, "pillar" of Hollywood's Asian-American community, honored at Academy Museum* [online]. The Hollywood Reporter. Available from: https://www.hollywoodreporter.com/movies/movie-news/janet-yang-honored-academy-museum-1235169764 [Accessed 22 Nov. 2022].

6. Grady, C. (2019). *Sandra Oh made history 3 times at the Golden Globes* [online]. Vox. Available from: https://www.vox.com/culture/2019/1/7/18171587/sandra-oh-golden-globes-2019-history-milestones.
7. allkpop. (n.d.). *"Rolling Stone" "BLACKPINK the world's biggest girl group continues their reign as the most followed music act in YouTube History" after surpassing 75 Million subscribers* [online]. Available from: https://www.allkpop.com/article/2022/06/rolling-stone-blackpink-the-worlds-biggest-girl-group-continues-their-reign-as-the-most-followed-music-act-in-youtube-history-after-surpassing-75-million-subscribers [Accessed 22 Nov. 2022].
8. Sarkar, S. (2022). *Meet Savitri Jindal, 72-year-old Asia's richest woman with net worth of $18 billion* [online]. thelogicalindian.com. Available from: https://thelogicalindian.com/trending/savitri-jindal-asias-richest-woman-36800 [Accessed 22 Nov. 2022].
9. NBC News. (n.d.). *Asian American women fall off by 80% at corporate leadership levels, a new report says* [online]. Available from: https://www.nbcnews.com/news/asian-america/asian-american-women-fall-80-corporate-leadership-levels-new-report-sa-rcna46546.

Resource List

The Joy Luck Club: https://www.goodreads.com/book/show/7763.The_Joy_Luck_Club

Asian Women Who BossUp: https://bit.ly/SYC-Shop

International Women of Color Who BossUp: https://amzn.to/3SJQT4Y

Asian Women Trailblazers Who BossUp: https://amzn.to/3No7SJ8

My Journey: The Story of an Unexpected Leader: https://amzn.to/3fgYBWG

Partner Track: https://amzn.to/3FyRfID

Rise: A Pop History of Asian America from the Nineties to Now: https://amzn.to/3sP5RvL

The Visibility Mindset: https://amzn.to/3DLxz2X

Dreaming of Gold, Dreaming of Home: https://amzn.to/3gVzHwa

American Sutra: https://amzn.to/3Fum0hT

Empire of Care: https://amzn.to/3DNFWex

Bengali Harlem and the Lost Histories of South Asian America: https://amzn.to/3SO22Sf

The Color of Success: https://amzn.to/3FrjtFj

Secret Pandemic: https://amzn.to/3DjDxGV

The Woman Warrior: https://amzn.to/3NkdFze

Angel Island: Immigrant Gateway to America: https://amzn.to/3sMdGm9

Crazy Rich Asians: https://amzn.to/3DLRn6r

Arranged Marriage: https://amzn.to/3Nhtnex

First They Killed My Father: A Daughter of Cambodia Remembers: https://amzn.to/3Fq0Z86

Asian American Histories of the United States: https://amzn.to/3zuYEF6

Acknowledgments

FIRST OFF, I never thought in my lifetime that I would write a full-length book, but this has been one of the best experiences in my entire life. The process was definitely a huge learning experience for me, and I am grateful to have been able to write a book that can change the way women are seen in leadership.

I would love to thank my family for their never-ending support: my mom, dad; my sisters Phoebe, Mathilda, and Ellen; my brother-in-law Roger; my nieces Mehgan and Shanaia; and my nephews Nolan and Jonah. You guys have been there through everything and have always stood by me even if you didn't understand what I was doing. Just being there has made a huge impact in my life and I am grateful to have you as my family.

To my friends Maureen, Aileen, Nicole, Mae, and Sabrina: I want to say thank you for being my best girlfriends a girl can ever have. You have been there through the craziest times of my life and have never left my side. Thank you for always sticking by me, no matter what the circumstances are.

To my WLG barkada, Diane, Melissa, Jovita, Khonie, Celina, and Lynel, I have known you girls since our SHS-G days, and

I am so grateful we have been able to keep in touch as much as we can through the different time zones we live in. Thank you always for being there for me through the years; I don't know what I would do without you.

To my #WomenWhoBossUp ladies, thank you for always encouraging me to #BossUp in my journey. You are the reason I keep moving forward. To Tam, I want to thank you for creating such an amazing movement and for believing in me at a time when I couldn't believe in myself. I am so grateful for everything you have done and for creating such an amazing community of Boss Ladies who are changing the world for the better. Thank you for your guidance, mentorship, and friendship. Without you and the community, this book would never have happened.

Last but not the least, a big thank you to YOU (Yes, you) for your support. Without you, none of this could have happened. I don't believe that anything is self-made. I know you have contributed to this whether it was listening to my podcast or reading this book. So thank you for your belief in me and my vision to create a positive impact in this world. Always know that wherever you may be in your journey, I am always rooting for you!

About the Author

Sheena Yap Chan is a keynote speaker, podcaster, consultant, and author on building self-confidence. She currently inspires women through her award-winning podcast called *The Tao of Self-Confidence*, where she interviews Asian women about their inner journey to self-confidence. Her mission is to help Asian women boost their confidence to live their authentic selves, help Asian women create a voice in the world, and create a stronger representation for Asian women. Sheena has been featured on MindValley, NBC, FOX, *Manila Times*, and more. She is also among the Top 100 Filipinos to follow on LinkedIn for inspiration and learning in 2021. She is also the coauthor of the international bestselling book, *Asian Women Who BossUp*.

Index